studysync®

Reading & Writing Companion

In Pursuit

studysync

studysync.com

Send all inquiries to:
BookheadEd Learning, LLC
610 Daniel Young Drive
Sonoma, CA 95476

8 9 LWI 21 20   C

STUDENT GUIDE

GETTING STARTED

Welcome to the StudySync Reading and Writing Companion! In this booklet, you will find a collection of readings based on the theme of the unit you are studying. As you work through the readings, you will be asked to answer questions and perform a variety of tasks designed to help you closely analyze and understand each text selection. Read on for an explanation of each section of this booklet.

CORE ELA TEXTS

In each Core ELA Unit you will read texts and text excerpts that share a common theme, despite their different genres, time periods, and authors. Each reading encourages a closer look with questions and a short writing assignment.

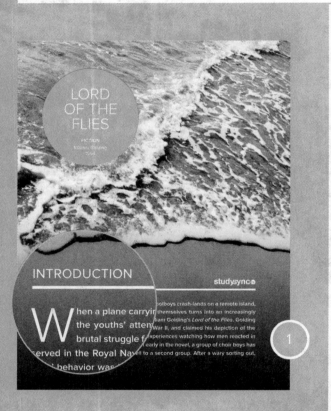

INTRODUCTION

An Introduction to each text provides historical context for your reading as well as information about the author. You will also learn about the genre of the excerpt and the year in which it was written.

FIRST READ

During your first reading of each excerpt, you should just try to get a general idea of the content and message of the reading. Don't worry if there are parts you don't understand or words that are unfamiliar to you. You'll have an opportunity later to dive deeper into the text.

NOTES

Many times, while working through the activities after each text, you will be asked to **annotate** or **make annotations** about what you are reading. This means that you should highlight or underline words in the text and use the "Notes" column to make comments or jot down any questions you may have. You may also want to note any unfamiliar vocabulary words here.

4 THINK QUESTIONS

These questions will ask you to start thinking critically about the text, asking specific questions about its purpose, and making connections to your prior knowledge and reading experiences. To answer these questions, you should go back to the text and draw upon specific evidence that you find there to support your responses. You will also begin to explore some of the more challenging vocabulary words used in the excerpt.

5 CLOSE READ & FOCUS QUESTIONS

After you have completed the First Read, you will then be asked to go back and read the excerpt more closely and critically. Before you begin your Close Read, you should read through the Focus Questions to get an idea of the concepts you will want to focus on during your second reading. You should work through the Focus Questions by making annotations, highlighting important concepts, and writing notes or questions in the "Notes" column. Depending on instructions from your teacher, you may need to respond online or use a separate piece of paper to start expanding on your thoughts and ideas.

6 WRITING PROMPT

Your study of each excerpt or selection will end with a writing assignment. To complete this assignment, you should use your notes, annotations, and answers to both the Think and Focus Questions. Be sure to read the prompt carefully and address each part of it in your writing assignment.

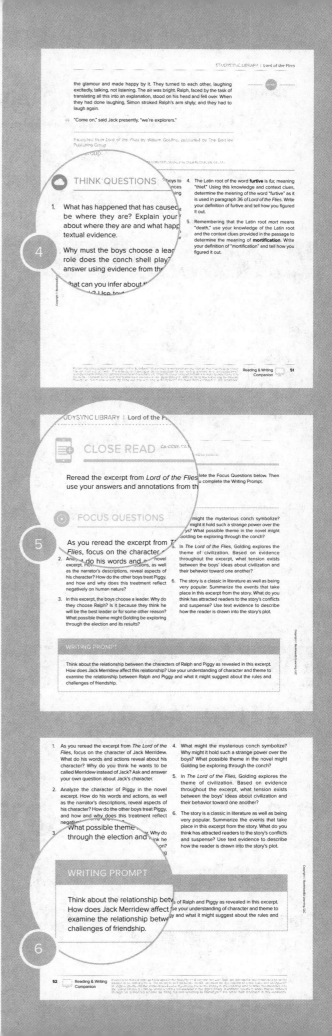

ENGLISH LANGUAGE DEVELOPMENT TEXTS

The English Language Development texts and activities take a closer look at the language choices that authors make to communicate their ideas. Individual and group activities will help develop your understanding of each text.

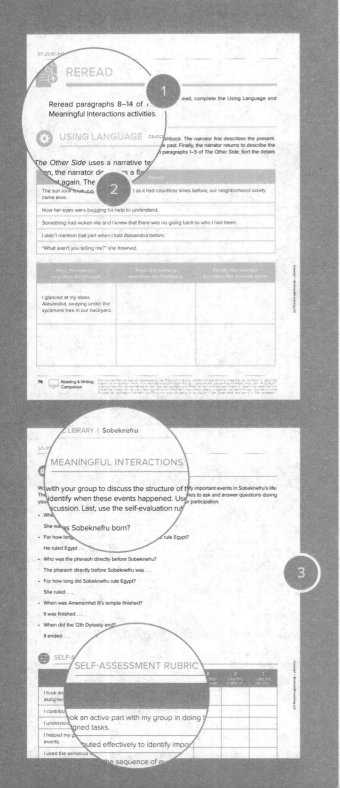

1 REREAD

After you have completed the First Read, you will have two additional opportunities to revisit portions of the excerpt more closely. The directions for each reread will specify which paragraphs or sections you should focus on.

2 USING LANGUAGE

These questions will ask you to analyze the author's use of language and conventions in the text. You may be asked to write in sentence frames, fill in a chart, or you may simply choose between multiple-choice options. To answer these questions, you should read the exercise carefully and go back in the text as necessary to accurately complete the activity.

3 MEANINGFUL INTERACTIONS & SELF-ASSESSMENT RUBRIC

After each reading, you will participate in a group activity or discussion with your peers. You may be provided speaking frames to guide your discussions or writing frames to support your group work. To complete these activities, you should revisit the excerpt for textual evidence and support. When you finish, use the Self-Assessment Rubric to evaluate how well you participated and collaborated.

EXTENDED WRITING PROJECT

The Extended Writing Project is your opportunity to explore the theme of each unit in a longer written work. You will draw information from your readings, research, and own life experiences to complete the assignment.

1 WRITING PROJECT

After you have read all of the unit text selections, you will move on to a writing project. Each project will guide you through the process of writing an argumentative, narrative, informative, or literary analysis essay. Student models and graphic organizers will provide guidance and help you organize your thoughts as you plan and write your essay. Throughout the project, you will also study and work on specific writing skills to help you develop different portions of your writing.

2 WRITING PROCESS STEPS

There are five steps in the writing process: **Prewrite, Plan, Draft, Revise,** and **Edit, Proofread, and Publish.** During each step, you will form and shape your writing project so that you can effectively express your ideas. Lessons focus on one step at a time, and you will have the chance to receive feedback from your peers and teacher.

3 WRITING SKILLS

Each Writing Skill lesson focuses on a specific strategy or technique that you will use during your writing project. The lessons begin by analyzing a student model or mentor text, and give you a chance to learn and practice the skill on its own. Then, you will have the opportunity to apply each new skill to improve the writing in your own project.

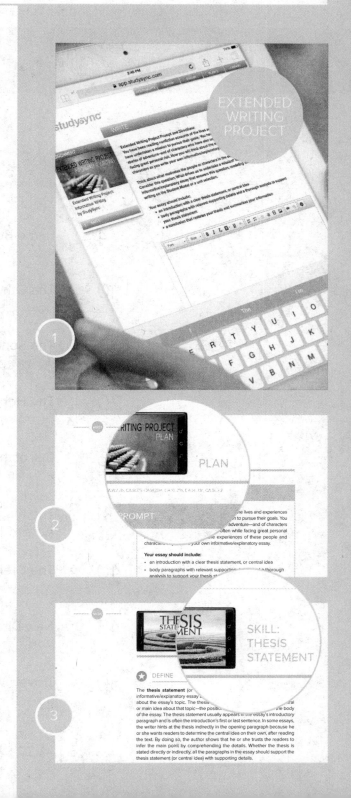

Reading & Writing Companion

In Pursuit

TEXTS

Reading & Writing
Companion

ENGLISH LANGUAGE DEVELOPMENT TEXTS

EXTENDED WRITING PROJECT

135

Text Fulfillment through StudySync

Please note that excerpts and passages in the StudySync® library and this workbook are intended as touchstones to generate interest in an author's work. The excerpts and passages do not substitute for the reading of entire texts, and StudySync® strongly recommends that students seek out and purchase the whole literary or informational work in order to experience it as the author intended. Links to online resellers are available in our digital library. In addition, complete works may be ordered through an authorized reseller by filling out and returning to StudySync® the order form enclosed in this workbook.

BARRIO BOY

NON-FICTION
Ernesto Galarza
1971

INTRODUCTION

Ernesto Galarza was a Mexican-American union leader and writer who spent most of his life fighting for the rights of farm workers. In *Barrio Boy*, Galarza tells the story of how he immigrated to California and successfully navigated the public school system. The excerpt is about Galarza's first experience in an American school.

"...there was a sign on the door in both Spanish and English: 'Principal.'"

FIRST READ

From Part Four: Life in the Lower Part of Town

1   The two of us walked south on Fifth Street one morning to the corner of Q Street and turned right. Half of the block was occupied by the Lincoln School. It was a three-story wooden building, with two wings that gave it the shape of a double-T connected by a central hall. It was a new building, painted yellow, with a shingled roof that was not like the red tile of the school in Mazatlán. I noticed other differences, none of them very reassuring.

2   We walked up the wide staircase hand in hand and through the door, which closed by itself. A mechanical contraption screwed to the top shut it behind us quietly.

3   Up to this point the adventure of enrolling me in the school had been carefully rehearsed. Mrs. Dodson had told us how to find it and we had circled it several times on our walks. Friends in the *barrio* explained that the director was called a principal, and that it was a lady and not a man. They assured us that there was always a person at the school who could speak Spanish.

4   Exactly as we had been told, there was a sign on the door in both Spanish and English: "Principal." We crossed the hall and entered the office of Miss Nettie Hopley.

5   Miss Hopley was at a roll-top desk to one side, sitting in a swivel chair that moved on wheels. There was a sofa against the opposite wall, flanked by two windows and a door that opened on a small balcony. Chairs were set around a table and framed pictures hung on the walls of a man with long white hair and another with a sad face and a black beard.

6   The principal half turned in the swivel chair to look at us over the pinch glasses crossed on the ridge of her nose. To do this she had to duck her head slightly as if she were about to step through a low doorway.

Copyright © BookheadEd Learning, LLC

7   What Miss Hopley said to us we did not know but we saw in her eyes a warm welcome and when she took off her glasses and straightened up she smiled wholeheartedly, like Mrs. Dodson. We were, of course, saying nothing, only catching the friendliness of her voice and the sparkle in her eyes while she said words we did not understand. She signaled us to the table. Almost tiptoeing across the office, I **maneuvered** myself to keep my mother between me and the gringo lady. In a matter of seconds I had to decide whether she was a possible friend or a **menace**. We sat down.

8   Then Miss Hopley did a **formidable** thing. She stood up. Had she been standing when we entered she would have seemed tall. But rising from her chair she soared. And what she carried up and up with her was a buxom superstructure, firm shoulders, a straight sharp nose, full cheeks slightly molded by a curved line along the nostrils, thin lips that moved like steel springs, and a high forehead topped by hair gathered in a bun. Miss Hopley was not a giant in body but when she **mobilized** it to a standing position she seemed a match for giants. I decided I liked her.

9   She strode to a door in the far corner of the office, opened it and called a name. A boy of about ten years appeared in the doorway. He sat down at one end of the table. He was brown like us, a plump kid with shiny black hair combed straight back, neat, cool, and faintly obnoxious.

10   Miss Hopley joined us with a large book and some papers in her hand. She, too, sat down and the questions and answers began by way of our **interpreter**. My name was Ernesto. My mother's name was Henriqueta. My birth certificate was in San Blas. Here was my last report card from the Escuela Municipal Numero 3 para Varones of Mazatlán, and so forth. Miss Hopley put things down in the book and my mother signed a card.

11   As long as the questions continued, Doña Henriqueta could stay and I was secure. Now that they were over, Miss Hopley saw her to the door, dismissed our interpreter and without further ado took me by the hand and strode down the hall to Miss Ryan's first grade.

12   Miss Ryan took me to a seat at the front of the room, into which I shrank—the better to survey her. She was, to skinny, somewhat runty me, of a withering height when she patrolled the class. And when I least expected it, there she was, crouching by my desk, her blond radiant face level with mine, her voice patiently maneuvering me over the awful **idiocies** of the English language.

13   During the next few weeks Miss Ryan overcame my fears of tall, energetic teachers as she bent over my desk to help me with a word in the pre-primer. Step by step, she loosened me and my classmates from the safe **anchorage** of the desks for recitations at the blackboard and consultations at her desk.

Copyright © BookheadEd Learning, LLC

Frequently she burst into happy announcements to the whole class. "Ito can read a sentence," and small Japanese Ito, squint-eyed and shy, slowly read aloud while the class listened in wonder: "Come, Skipper, come. Come and run." The Korean, Portuguese, Italian, and Polish first graders had similar moments of glory, no less shining than mine the day I conquered "butterfly," which I had been persistently pronouncing in standard Spanish as boo-ter-flee. "Children," Miss Ryan called for attention. "Ernesto has learned how to pronounce *butterfly!*" And I proved it with a perfect imitation of Miss Ryan. From that celebrated success, I was soon able to match Ito's progress as a sentence reader with "Come, butterfly, come fly with me."

14   Like Ito and several other first graders who did not know English, I received private lessons from Miss Ryan in the closet, a narrow hall off the classroom with a door at each end. Next to one of these doors Miss Ryan placed a large chair for herself and a small one for me. Keeping an eye on the class through the open door she read with me about sheep in the meadow and a frightened chicken going to see the king, coaching me out of my phonetic ruts in words like pasture, *bow-wow-wow, hay,* and *pretty,* which to my Mexican ear and eye had so many unnecessary sounds and letters. She made me watch her lips and then close my eyes as she repeated words I found hard to read. When we came to know each other better, I tried interrupting to tell Miss Ryan how we said it in Spanish. It didn't work. She only said "oh" and went on with *pasture, bow-wow-wow,* and *pretty.* It was as if in that closet we were both discovering together the secrets of the English language and grieving together over the tragedies of Bo-Peep. The main reason I was graduated with honors from the first grade was that I had fallen in love with Miss Ryan. Her radiant, no-nonsense character made us either afraid not to love her or love her so we would not be afraid, I am not sure which. It was not only that we sensed she was with it, but also that she was with us.

15   Like the first grade, the rest of the Lincoln School was a sampling of the lower part of town where many races made their home. My pals in the second grade were Kazushi, whose parents spoke only Japanese; Matti, a skinny Italian boy; and Manuel, a fat Portuguese who would never get into a fight but wrestled you to the ground and just sat on you. Our assortment of nationalities included Koreans, Yugoslavs, Poles, Irish, and home-grown Americans.

16   Miss Hopley and her teachers never let us forget why we were at Lincoln: for those who were alien, to become good Americans; for those who were so born, to accept the rest of us. Off the school grounds we traded the same insults we heard from our elders. On the playground we were sure to be marched up to the principal's office for calling someone a wop, a chink, a dago, or a greaser. The school was not so much a melting pot as a griddle where Miss Hopley and her helpers warmed knowledge into us and roasted racial hatreds out of us.

NOTES

17 At Lincoln, making us into Americans did not mean scrubbing away what made us originally foreign. The teachers called us as our parents did, or as close as they could pronounce our names in Spanish or Japanese. No one was ever scolded or punished for speaking in his native tongue on the playground. Matti told the class about his mother's down quilt, which she had made in Italy with the fine feathers of a thousand geese. Encarnación acted out how boys learned to fish in the Philippines. I astounded the third grade with the story of my travels on a stagecoach, which nobody else in the class had seen except in the museum at Sutter's Fort. After a visit to the Crocker Art Gallery and its collection of heroic paintings of the golden age of California, someone showed a silk scroll with a Chinese painting. Miss Hopley herself had a way of expressing wonder over these matters before a class, her eyes wide open until they popped slightly. It was easy for me to feel that becoming a proud American, as she said we should, did not mean feeling ashamed of being a Mexican.

From BARRIO BOY by Ernesto Galarza. Copyright © 1971 by Ernesto Galarza. Used by permission of University of Notre Dame Press.

THINK QUESTIONS CA-CCSS: CA.RI.7.1, CA.L.7.4a, CA.L.7.4d

1. What is the most important idea in the first paragraph? Cite specific evidence from the selection or make inferences drawn from the text to support your answer.

2. How do Miss Hopley's actions in paragraphs 7 and 8 help Ernesto decide whether the principal is a possible "friend or a menace"? What does he decide about her? Cite specific evidence from the text to support your answer.

3. How does the author's word choice in paragraph 12 that begins, "Miss Ryan took me to a seat at the front of the room," help readers understand how Ernesto was feeling on his first day in Miss Ryan's class? Cite three examples from the text to support your response.

4. Which context clues helped you determine the meaning of the word **formidable** as it is used in paragraph 8 of Barrio Boy? Write your definition of "formidable" and indicate the clues that helped you figure out the meaning of the word.

5. Which context clues in the passage helped you figure out the meaning of **mobilized**, in paragraph 8? Write your definition of the word "mobilized." Tell how you figured out the meaning of the word. Then use a print or an online dictionary to confirm the definition.

CLOSE READ

CA-CCSS: CA.RI.7.1, CA.RI.7.2, CA.RI.7.3, CA.RI.7.4, CA.L.7.5a, CA.L.7.5c, CA.W.7.2a, CA.W.7.2b, CA.W.7.2c, CA.W.7.2d, CA.W.7.2e, CA.W.7.2f, CA.W.7.5, CA.W.7.6, CA.W.7.10

Reread the excerpt from *Barrio Boy*. As you reread, complete the Focus Questions below. Then use your answers and annotations from the questions to help you complete the Writing Prompt.

FOCUS QUESTIONS

1. As you reread the excerpt from *Barrio Boy*, remember that like most authors, Galarza never explicitly states the central ideas. Instead, it is up to the reader to infer the central ideas by drawing inferences from what is stated directly in the text. Reread paragraph 17. What details in the paragraph support the opening sentence: "At Lincoln, making us into Americans did not mean scrubbing away what made us originally foreign"? Make annotations about how this sentence might state a central idea.

2. An author's word choice can impact a reader's understanding of a passage. How effective is the author's choice of the word "soared" to describe Miss Hopley in paragraph 8? Make annotations noting what the word connotes about the principal. How does the author's deliberate use of this word and other words in the paragraph help readers to see Miss Hopley through the eyes of a small boy?

3. In paragraph 16, Galarza recollects that the "school was not so much a melting pot as a griddle where Miss Hopley and her helpers warmed knowledge into us and roasted racial hatreds out of us." Highlight this powerful metaphor in the text. What idea about the school does it connote? Then make annotations noting the evidence in the paragraph that supports the comparison being made in the metaphor.

4. Reread the first and last paragraph of the excerpt. How has Ernesto changed from the beginning of the selection to the end? Make annotations jotting down words and phrases that describe him early on and then later in the excerpt. Then note two central ideas that are developed over the course of the text.

5. In paragraph 12, Ernesto credits Miss Ryan with "maneuvering . . . [him] over the awful idiocies of the English language." Find and highlight textual evidence in paragraphs 13 and 14 to demonstrate how Miss Ryan accomplishes that mission. Then write a sentence summarizing the process. Include a strong central idea in your summary sentence.

WRITING PROMPT

What is the excerpt from *Barrio Boy* all about? How does Ernesto change from the beginning of the excerpt to the end? What do the details in the text have in common? Use your understanding of central (or main) ideas to determine two central ideas that are developed over the course of the text. Then use these central ideas and the details that support them to write an objective summary of the text in your own words. Use transitions to clarify relationships among your ideas. Support your writing with textual evidence and precise language that fully explains your conclusions. Establish a formal style and be sure not to include your feelings, opinions, or judgments. Provide a conclusion that logically follows the information you have presented.

Please note that excerpts and passages in the StudySync® library and this workbook are intended as touchstones to generate interest in an author's work. The excerpts and passages do not substitute for the reading of entire texts, and StudySync® strongly recommends that students seek out and purchase the whole literary or informational work in order to experience it as the author intended. Links to online resellers are available in our digital library. In addition, complete works may be ordered through an authorized reseller by filling out and returning to StudySync® the order form enclosed in this workbook.

Reading & Writing Companion

9

THE OTHER SIDE OF THE SKY

NON-FICTION
Farah Ahmedi and
Tanim Ansary
2006

INTRODUCTION

Farah Ahmedi's memoir *The Other Side of the Sky* is a testament to the power of the human spirit. Missing a leg after stepping on a land mine when she was seven, and with her father and brothers dead from a rocket attack, Ahmedi and her mother decide to flee their home in Kabul in search of a better life. This excerpt from "Escape from Afghanistan" describes their efforts to make it across the border and into Pakistan.

"There was nothing here, no town, no hotel, no buildings, just the desert."

FIRST READ

From: Escape from Afghanistan

1   The gate to Pakistan was closed, and I could see that the Pakistani border guards were letting no one through. People were pushing and shoving and jostling up against that gate, and the guards were driving them back. As we got closer, the crowd thickened, and I could hear the roar and clamor at the gate. The Afghans were yelling something, and the Pakistanis were yelling back. My mother was clutching her side and gasping for breath, trying to keep up. I felt desperate to get through, because the sun was setting, and if we got stuck here, what were we going to do? Where would we stay? There was nothing here, no town, no hotel, no buildings, just the desert.

2   Yet we had no real chance of getting through. Big strong men were running up to the gate in vain. The guards had clubs, and they had carbines, too, which they turned around and used as weapons. Again and again, the crowd surged toward the gate and the guards drove them back with their sticks and clubs, swinging and beating until the crowd receded. And after that, for the next few minutes, on our side of the border, people milled about and muttered and stoked their own impatience and worked up their rage, until gradually the crowd gathered strength and surged against that gate again, only to be swept back.

3   We never even got close to the front. We got caught up in the thinning rear end of crowd, and even so, we were part of each wave, pulled forward, driven back. It was hard for me to keep my footing, and my mother was clutching my arm now, just hanging on, just trying to stay close to me, because the worst thing would have been if we had gotten separated. Finally, I saw that it was no use. We were only risking injury. We drifted back, out of the crowd. In the thickening dusk we could hear the dull roar of people still trying to get past the border guards, but we receded into the desert, farther and farther back from the border gate.

4   Night was falling, and we were stranded out there in the open.

· · ·

5   On that second day, however, I learned that it was all a question of money. Someone told me about this, and then I watched closely and saw that it was true. Throughout the day, while some of the guards confronted the crowds, a few others lounged over to the side. People approached them quietly. Money changed hands, and the guards then let those people quietly through a small door to the side.

6   Hundreds could have flowed through the main gate had it been opened, but only one or two could get through the side door at a time. The fact that the guards were taking bribes did us no good whatsoever. We did not have the money to pay them. What little we had we would need to get from Peshawar to Quetta. And so the second day passed.

7   At the end of that day we found ourselves camping near a friendly family. We struck up a conversation with them. The woman told us that her husband, Ghulam Ali, had gone to look for another way across the border. He was checking out a goat path that supposedly went over the mountains several miles northeast of the border station. If one could get to Pakistan safely by that route, he would come back for his family. "You can go with us," the woman said.

8   Later that night her husband showed up. "It works," he said. "Smugglers use that path, and they bribe the guards to leave it unguarded. Of course, we don't want to run into any smugglers, either, but if we go late at night, we should be fine."

9   His wife then told him our story, and Ghulam Ali took pity on us. "Yes, of course you can come with us," he said. "But you have had two hard days. You will need some rest before you attempt this mountain crossing. Spend tonight here and sleep well, knowing that you will have nothing to do tomorrow except lounge around, rest, and catch your breath. Tomorrow, do not throw yourself against those border guards again. Let your only work be the gathering of your strength. Then tomorrow night we will all go over the mountain together, with God's grace. I will show you the way. If God wills it, we will follow that smugglers' path to safety. You and your mother are in my care now."

10 So we spent the whole next day there. It was terribly warm and we had no water, but we walked a little way and found a mosque that refugees like us had built over the years, so that people waiting to get across the border would have a place to say their prayers. We got some water to drink at the

Copyright © BookheadEd Learning, LLC

mosque, and we said *namaz* there too. Somehow we obtained a little bit of bread as well. I can't remember how that turned up, but there it was, and we ate it. We sustained our strength. After sunset we lay down just as if were going to spend another night. In fact, I did fall asleep for a while. Long after dark—or early the next morning, to be exact, before the sun came up—that man shook us awake. "It's time," he said.

11   We got up and performed our **ablutions** quickly in the darkness, with just sand because that's allowed when you have no access to water. We said our prayers. Then Ghulam Ali began to march into the darkness with his family, and we trudged along silently behind them. After several miles the path began to climb, and my mother began to wheeze. Her asthma was pretty bad at this point, poor thing. No doubt, her anxiety made it worse, but in such circumstances how could she rid herself of anxiety? It was no use knowing that her difficulty was rooted in anxiety, just as it was no use knowing that we could have moved more quickly if we had possessed wings. Life is what it is. The path over that mountain was not actually very long, only a couple of miles. Steep as it was, we could have gotten over in little more than an hour if not for my mother. Because of her, we had to pause every few minutes, so our journey took many hours.

12   I myself hardly felt the exertion. I was walking quite well that day, quite athletically. I had that good **prosthetic** leg from Germany. The foot was a little worn by then, but not enough to slow me down. Thinking back, I'm puzzled, actually. How did I scale that mountain so easily? How did I climb down the other side? These days I find it hard to clamber up two or three flights of stairs, even. I don't know what made me so **supple** and strong that day, but I felt no hardship, no anxiety or fear, just concentration and intensity. Perhaps my mother's problems distracted me from my own. That might account for it. Perhaps desperation gave me energy and made me forget the **rigor** of the climb. Well, whatever the reason, I scrambled up like a goat. The family we were following had a girl only a bit younger than me, and she was moving slowly. Her family used my example to chide her. They kept saying, "Look at that girl. She's missing a leg, and yet she's going faster than you. Why can't you keep up? Hurry now!"

13   That Ghulam Ali was certainly a good man, so patient with us and so **compassionate**. He had never seen us before, and yet when he met us, he said, "I will help you." That's the thing about life. You never know when and where you will encounter a spot of human decency. I have felt alone in this world at times; I have known long periods of being no one. But then, without warning, a person like Ghulam Ali just turns up and says, "I see you. I am on your side." Strangers have been kind to me when it mattered most. That sustains a person's hope and faith.

Excerpted from *The Other Side of the Sky* by Farah Ahmedi, published by Simon & Schuster.

 THINK QUESTIONS CA-CCSS: CA.RI.7.1, CA.L.7.4a, CA.L.7.4d, CA.L.7.5b

1. Why were Ahmedi and her mother near the gate to the Pakistani border? Why couldn't they get any nearer to the gate? Why was Ahmedi desperate to get through the border crossing to Pakistan? Cite specific evidence from paragraphs 1 and 2 of the text to support your answer.

2. What did Ahmedi learn on the second day about why a few people were being allowed to enter Pakistan? Why didn't this knowledge help her and her mother? What happened on the night of the second day to give Ahmedi hope? Cite specific evidence from paragraphs 5–9 to support your response.

3. What physical challenges did Ahmedi and her mother face as they crossed the mountain? Why was Ahmedi puzzled by her own physical abilities during the mountain crossing? What does she suppose is the reason for her ability to scale the mountain so easily? Support your answers with specific evidence from paragraphs 11 and 12 of the text.

4. How does sentence 8 in paragraph 12—"These days I find it hard to clamber up two or three flights of stairs, even"—help you understand the meaning of the word **supple** in the next sentence? "I don't know what made me so supple and strong that day, but I felt no hardship, no anxiety or fear, just concentration and intensity." Cite specific evidence from the text to support your answer.

5. Use the context clues provided in the last paragraph to determine the meaning of the word **compassionate**. Write your definition of "compassionate" and indicate the context clues that helped you infer the meaning of the word. Check a print or an online dictionary to confirm your definition.

CLOSE READ

CA-CCSS: CA.RI.7.1, CA.RI.7.2, CA.RI.7.3, CA.RI.7.4, CA.W.7.2b, CA.W.7.2c, CA.W.7.2d, CA.W.7.2f, CA.W.7.5, CA.W.7.6, CA.W.7.10, CA.L.7.4a, CA.L.7.6

Reread the excerpt from *The Other Side of the Sky*. As you reread, complete the Focus Questions below. Then use your answers and annotations from the questions to help you complete the Writing Prompt.

FOCUS QUESTIONS

1. The Afghans surge toward the gate, are driven back, and then mill about, stoke their impatience and rage, and surge forward again. How might this recurring action have unintentionally helped the people who were slipping money to the guards? Highlight the evidence in the text that supports your inference. Then annotate your answer.

2. What did Ghulam Ali instruct Ahmedi and her mother to do in paragraph 9? What can you infer about the next day's journey from his advice? Highlight Ghulam Ali's instructions and annotate your answer.

3. In paragraph 10, what can you infer about the meaning of the word *namaz* from the context clues in the paragraph? Highlight the specific clues in the text that helped you infer the meaning of the word, and annotate your answer.

4. In paragraph 12, Ahmedi writes, "These days I find it hard to clamber up two or three flights of stairs, even." What can you infer from this statement? How does this inference help you understand why Ahmedi was puzzled that she could scale the mountain so easily? Annotate how these thoughts contribute to the development of a central idea within the passage.

5. As you reread the selection, think about what the text says explicitly and what you can infer. In the first paragraph, what factors drive Ahmedi to accomplish her mission of getting across the border into Pakistan? Highlight specific textual evidence to support your ideas, and annotate inferences that you can draw from this textual evidence.

WRITING PROMPT

This excerpt from *The Other Side of the Sky* assumes a certain level of understanding about the geography, history, current events, and way of life of the Afghan people, including Islamic religious practices, that readers may not have. What examples of unfamiliar vocabulary, geography, history or current events, and the Islamic way of life might have presented problems for you (or other readers) and hindered a full understanding of the text? What explicitly stated details helped you draw inferences from the text so that you could better understand it? Write a brief informative/explanatory essay to explain how you figured things out in the text. Cite specific evidence and vocabulary from the text to support your writing. Use transitions to clarify relationships among your ideas, and conclude with a statement that supports the information and central ideas in your essay.

THE SONG OF WANDERING AENGUS

POETRY
William Butler Yeats
1899

INTRODUCTION

In Irish mythology, Aengus is the god of love and youth. He falls in love with a maiden in a dream, finds her, and the two turn into swans. In Yeats's poem, Aengus is mortal, on a quest to find the "glimmering girl" whom he met by chance and who has vanished. His wandering, a life-long search for the object of his desires, represents the human inclination and yearning for love, knowledge, and perfection.

"It had become a glimmering girl…"

 FIRST READ

NOTES

1 I went out to the hazel wood,
2 Because a fire was in my head,
3 And cut and peeled a hazel wand,
4 And hooked a berry to a thread;
5 And when white moths were on the wing,
6 And moth-like stars were **flickering** out,
7 I dropped the berry in a stream
8 And caught a little silver trout.

9 When I had laid it on the floor
10 I went to blow the fire a-flame,
11 But something **rustled** on the floor,
12 And someone called me by my name:
13 It had become a **glimmering** girl
14 With apple blossom in her hair
15 Who called me by my name and ran
16 And faded through the brightening air.

17 Though I am old with **wandering**
18 Through hollow lands and hilly lands,
19 I will find out where she has gone,
20 And kiss her lips and take her hands;
21 And walk among long **dappled** grass,
22 And **pluck** till time and times are done,
23 The silver apples of the moon,
24 The golden apples of the sun.

THINK QUESTIONS   CA-CCSS: CA.RL.7.1, CA.L.7.4a, CA.L.7.4d, CA.SL.7.1a, CA.SL.7.1d, CA.SL.7.3

1. Where did the "glimmering girl" come from? Cite specific evidence from the text to support your response.

2. How do you know that a lot of time has passed between the events in the first two stanzas and the events in the last stanza? Cite specific textual evidence.

3. Cite specific examples of repetition in the last stanza. How do the repeated words and phrases help readers understand the speaker's commitment to searching for the object of his desire?

4. Use context to determine the meaning of the word **flickering** as it is used in line 6 of "The Song of Wandering Aengus." Write your definition of "flickering" and cite specific context clues to explain how you determined its meaning.

5. Compare and contrast the meaning of **wandering** as it is used as an adjective in the title of the poem and as a noun in the first line of the third stanza. Cite specific evidence from the text. Then, look up the word in a print or online dictionary to confirm its meaning.

CLOSE READ
CA-CCSS: CA.RL.7.1, CA.RL.7.2, CA.RL.7.4, CA.L.7.5a, CA.W.7.2a, CA.W.7.2b, CA.W.7.2c, CA.W.7.2d, CA.W.7.2f, CA.W.7.4, CA.W.7.5, CA.W.7.6, CA.W.7.10

Reread the poem "The Song of Wandering Aengus." As you reread, complete the Focus Questions below. Then use your answers and annotations from the questions to help you complete the Writing Prompt.

 ## FOCUS QUESTIONS

1. As you reread "The Song of Wandering Aengus," highlight the metaphor in the first stanza that explains why the speaker went fishing. How does the metaphor indicate how the speaker is feeling? How does it suggest what he is hoping might happen? Make annotations citing textual evidence to explain your analysis.

2. Which simile in the first stanza indicates the time of day when the speaker goes fishing? Highlight the simile and make annotations citing textual evidence to explain your response.

3. Which terms in the second stanza are derived from the image of light? Analyze and highlight the image of "fire a-flame" in the second line, and explain its impact on the second stanza. Make annotations supporting your response with specific evidence from the text.

4. Think about the allusion (or reference) in the poem to the mythical Aengus. How might his search for the girl in his dream be similar to the speaker's search for his "dream girl" in the poem? How does this allusion to the mythical Aengus, the Celtic god of love, youth, and beauty, suggest the poem's theme? Make annotations providing textual support for your answer.

5. Highlight specific evidence in the last stanza that suggests what motivates the speaker to undertake a lifelong mission to find the "glimmering girl." Do you think he will ever stop looking for her? Think of your own theme statement for the poem, based on the idea of undertaking a mission to accomplish a goal. Make annotations providing textual support for your theme statement.

WRITING PROMPT

Think about the speaker's mission in "The Song of Wandering Aengus." How determined is he to complete his mission of finding his "dream girl"? This question can help you identify another theme in the poem. What theme is it? Write your response in the form of a clear statement of theme. Then support that theme with specific evidence from the text. Organize and explain how figurative language, allusion, and other poetic elements in the poem support the theme you have identifie[d]. Use transitions to show the relationships among these ideas, and conclude with a statemen[t] supports your information.

THE HOBBIT

FiCTION
J.R.R. Tolkien
1937

INTRODUCTION

Thirteen dwarves and the great wizard, Gandalf, have come to the home of a hobbit named Bilbo Baggins. The dwarves are embarking on a journey to claim their Mountain and their treasure, taken from them by Smaug, a dragon. For reasons unknown to the hobbit, the dwarves have the fourteenth member of their expedition. But when Thorin, the ...s that they "may never return," Bilbo collapses in a shrieking ...de of Bilbo's family will carry more weight—the comfort- the adventurous Tooks? And will an ancient map of the ...ecrets?

"There is a lot more in him than you guess..."

 FIRST READ

NOTES

From Chapter 1: An Unexpected Party

1 "Excitable little fellow," said Gandalf, as they sat down again. "Gets funny queer fits, but he is one of the best, one of the best—as fierce as a dragon in a pinch."

2 If you have ever seen a dragon in a pinch, you will realize that this was only poetical exaggeration applied to any hobbit, even to Old Took's great-granduncle Bullroarer, who was so huge (for a hobbit) that he could ride a horse. He charged the **ranks** of the goblins of Mount Gram in the Battle of the Green Fields, and knocked their king Golfimbul's head clean off with a wooden club. It sailed a hundred yards through the air and went down a rabbit hole, and in this way the battle was won and the game of Golf invented at the same moment.

3 In the meanwhile, however, Bullroarer's gentler descendant was reviving in the drawing-room. After a while and a drink he crept nervously to the door of the parlour. This is what he heard, Gloin speaking: "Humph!" (or some snort more or less like that). "Will he do, do you think? It is all very well for Gandalf to talk about this hobbit being fierce, but one shriek like that in a moment of excitement would be enough to wake the dragon and all his relatives, and kill the lot of us. I think it sounded more like fright than excitement! In fact, if it had not been for the sign on the door, I should have been sure we had come to the wrong house. As soon as I clapped eyes on the little fellow bobbing and puffing on the mat, I had my doubts. He looks more like a grocer than a burglar!"

4 Then Mr. Baggins turned the handle and went in. The Took side had won. He suddenly felt he would go without bed and breakfast to be thought fierce. As for little fellow bobbing on the mat it almost made him really fierce. Many a time afterwards the Baggins part regretted what he did now, and he said to himself: "Bilbo, you were a fool; you walked right in and put your foot in it."

Please note that excerpts and passages in the StudySync® library and this workbook are intended as touchstones to generate interest in an author's work. The excerpts and passages do not substitute for the reading of entire texts, and StudySync® strongly recommends that students seek out and purchase the whole literary or informational work in order to experience it as the author intended. Links to online resellers are available in our digital library. In addition, complete works may be ordered through an authorized reseller by filling out and returning to StudySync® the order form enclosed in this workbook.

Reading & Writing Companion

21

NOTES

5   "Pardon me," he said, "if I have overheard words that you were saying. I don't pretend to understand what you are talking about, or your reference to burglars, but I think I am right in believing" (this is what he called being on his dignity) "that you think I am no good. I will show you. I have no signs on my door—it was painted a week ago—, and I am quite sure you have come to the wrong house. As soon as I saw your funny faces on the door-step, I had my doubts. But treat it as the right one. Tell me what you want done, and I will try it, if I have to walk from here to the East of East and fight the wild Were-worms in the Last Desert. I had a great-great-great-granduncle once, Bullroarer Took, and—"

6   "Yes, yes, but that was long ago," said Gloin. "I was talking about you. And I assure you there is a mark on this door—the usual one in the trade, or used to be. Burglar wants a good job, plenty of Excitement and reasonable Reward, that's how it is usually read. You can say Expert Treasure-hunter instead of Burglar if you like. Some of them do. It's all the same to us. Gandalf told us that there was a man of the sort in these parts looking for a Job at once, and that he had arranged for a meeting here this Wednesday tea-time."

7   "Of course there is a mark," said Gandalf. "I put it there myself. For very good reasons. You asked me to find the fourteenth man for your expedition, and I chose Mr. Baggins. Just let any one say I chose the wrong man or the wrong house, and you can stop at thirteen and have all the bad luck you like, or go back to digging coal."

8   He scowled so angrily at Gloin that the dwarf huddled back in his chair; and when Bilbo tried to open his mouth to ask a question, he turned and frowned at him and stuck out his bushy eyebrows, till Bilbo shut his mouth tight with a snap.

9   "That's right," said Gandalf. "Let's have no more argument. I have chosen Mr. Baggins and that ought to be enough for all of you. If I say he is a Burglar, a Burglar he is, or will be when the time comes. There is a lot more in him than you guess, and a deal more than he has any idea of himself. You may (possibly) all live to thank me yet.

. . .

10   "Also," went on Gandalf, "I forgot to mention that with the map went a key, a small and curious key. Here it is!" he said, and handed to Thorin a key with a long barrel and **intricate** wards, made of silver. "Keep it safe!"

11   "Indeed I will," said Thorin, and he fastened it upon a fine chain that hung about his neck and under his jacket. "Now things begin to look more hopeful. This news alters them much for the better. So far we have had no clear idea

what to do. We thought of going East, as quiet and careful as we could, as far as the Long Lake. After that the trouble would begin—"

12   "A long time before that, if I know anything about the roads East," interrupted Gandalf.

13   "We might go from there up along the River Running," went on Thorin taking no notice, "and so to the ruins of Dale—the old town in the valley there, under the shadow of the Mountain. But we none of us liked the idea of the Front Gate. The river runs right out of it through the great cliff at the South of the Mountain, and out of it comes the dragon too—far too often, unless he has changed."

14   "That would be no good," said the wizard, "not without a mighty Warrior, even a Hero. I tried to find one; but warriors are busy fighting one another in distant lands, and in this neighbourhood heroes are scarce, or simply not to be found. Swords in these parts are mostly blunt, and axes are used for trees, and shields as cradles or dish-covers; and dragons are comfortably far-off (and therefore legendary). That is why I settled on burglary—especially when I remembered the existence of a Side-door. And here is our little Bilbo Baggins, the burglar, the chosen and selected burglar. So now let's get on and make some plans."

15   "Very well then," said Thorin, "supposing the burglar-expert gives us some ideas or suggestions." He turned with mock-politeness to Bilbo.

16   "First I should like to know a bit more about things," said he, feeling all confused and a bit shaky inside, but so far still Tookishly determined to go on with things. "I mean about the gold and the dragon, and all that, and how it got there, and who it belongs to, and so on and further."

17   "Bless me!" said Thorin, "haven't you got a map? and didn't you hear our song? and haven't we been talking about all this for hours?"

18   "All the same, I should like it all plain and clear," said he **obstinately,** putting on his business manner (usually reserved for people who tried to borrow money off him), and doing his best to appear wise and **prudent** and professional and live up to Gandalf's recommendation. "Also I should like to know about risks, out-of-pocket expenses, time required and **remuneration,** and so forth"—by which he meant: "What am I going to get out of it? and am I going to come back alive?"

. . .

19   After all the others had ordered their breakfasts without so much as a please (which annoyed Bilbo very much), they all got up. The hobbit had to find room

for them all, and filled all his spare-rooms and made beds on chairs and sofas, before he got them all stowed and went to his own little bed very tired and not altogether happy.

Excerpted from *The Hobbit* by J. R. R. Tolkien, published by Houghton Mifflin Harcourt.

 THINK QUESTIONS CA-CCSS: CA.RL.7.1, CA.L.7.4a, CA.SL.7.1c, CA.SL.7.4

1. Why does Gandalf think that Bilbo is right for the job of burglar? Cite specific evidence from paragraphs 1 and 9 to support your answer.

2. What are the two sides of Bilbo's personality? Cite specific evidence from the text, especially in paragraphs 4, 5, and 18 to support your answer.

3. Why does Gandalf think it is important to include Bilbo as the fourteenth member of the expedition? What can you infer from the evidence in paragraph 7 about embarking on an expedition with 13 members? Cite textual evidence.

4. Use context to determine the meaning of the word **prudent** as it is used in paragraph 18 of *The Hobbit*. Write your definition of "prudent" and explain your reasoning based on context clues.

5. Find the word **remuneration** in paragraph 18 of the excerpt. Write your definition of the word, and list the context clues that helped you determine its meaning. Check your definition in a print or digital dictionary to confirm the meaning you inferred.

CLOSE READ

CA-CCSS: CA.RL.7.1, CA.RL.7.3, CA.RL.7.4, CA.W.7.2a, CA.W.7.2b, CA.W.7.2c, CA.W.7.2f, CA.W.7.4, CA.W.7.5, CA.W.7.6, CA.W.7.10, CA.L.7.4c

Reread the excerpt from *The Hobbit*. As you reread, complete the Focus Questions below. Then use your answers and annotations from the questions to help you complete the Writing Prompt.

 FOCUS QUESTIONS

1. Reread paragraphs 1–4. How is one side of Bilbo's personality beginning to take over? Cite specific textual evidence from these paragraphs to support the idea that "[t]he Took side had won." Highlight the words, phrases, and sentences that support the idea that Bilbo is becoming strong and fierce. Make annotations recording your response.

2. What action sparks Gandalf's dialogue and behavior in paragraphs 7–9? What do Gandalf's words and actions reveal about his character? Why is it likely that Gandalf will influence the events of the plot? Make annotations recording evidence from the text to support your inferences and analysis.

3. Reread paragraphs 1–3. What is the setting of the story? Highlight words and phrases that indicate the time and the place. Make annotations describing the setting and answering these questions: How might the setting influence the characters in the text? How might it shape the events of the plot? Cite specific textual evidence to support your answers.

4. Reread paragraph 18 in the excerpt. Use your understanding of the strategies for analyzing a character to highlight adjectives and adverbs that describe Bilbo. Make annotations listing adjectives and adverbs and indicating in parentheses the part of speech of each word. Look in a print or digital dictionary to confirm the part of speech.

5. Reread paragraph 5. What can you infer about Bilbo's character from his dialogue? What drives him to undertake the mission? Highlight words and phrases that suggest he is determined to do what he must to join the expedition. Then draw an inference about how Bilbo will influence the events of the plot. Make annotations recording your answer.

WRITING PROMPT

Story elements—setting, character, and plot—interact. Therefore, characters in a story may influence the action of the plot, or the plot may influence the actions of the characters. How might the story element of character influence the events of the plot (or the conflict of the plot) in *The Hobbit?* For example, how might the two sides of Bilbo's personality—one excitable, nervous, and cautious, the other strong and fierce—impact the plot? Answer the question with a clear thesis statement. Draw inferences from the text, and support your writing with specific textual evidence. Organize your ideas, and use transitions to clarify and connect them. Write a strong conclusion that summarizes your ideas and "wraps up" your essay.

Please note that excerpts and passages in the StudySync® library and this workbook are intended as touchstones to generate interest in an author's work. The excerpts and passages do not substitute for the reading of entire texts, and StudySync® strongly recommends that students seek out and purchase the whole literary or informational work in order to experience it as the author intended. Links to online resellers are available in our digital library. In addition, complete works may be ordered through an authorized reseller by filling out and returning to StudySync® the order form enclosed in this workbook.

Reading & Writing Companion   **25**

CALL OF THE KLONDIKE

A TRUE GOLD RUSH ADVENTURE

NON-FICTION

David Meissner and
Kim Richardson
2013

INTRODUCTION

Call of the Klondike tells the story of Stanley Pearce and Marshall Bond, two men who organized one of the earliest expeditions of the Klondike Gold Rush. Authored in part by Pearce's great-great-nephew, the prospectors' account of hardship and adventure is told through primary source documents, including telegrams, letters, diary entries, and newspaper articles.

"Both groups of miners had found their gold in the same place..."

 FIRST READ

NOTES

From: Gold Fever Strikes

1   Stanley Pearce and Marshall Bond were in Seattle, Washington, when it happened. On July 17, 1897, sixty-eight rugged miners stepped off the S.S. *Portland* steamship and made their way through the excited crowd. They were carrying large sacks filled with the most precious metal in the world—gold.

2   Stanley Pearce described the scene this way: "Thousands of people in the public square watched the weather-beaten and hardy adventurers stagger into the express office with sacks of gold, gold in blankets, in oil cans, and even in moccasins."

3   Together, these miners brought back an astounding four thousand pounds of gold. It was worth nearly one million dollars, which, by today's standards, would be many times that amount. Three days earlier, miners on another ship, the S.S. *Excelsior,* had arrived in San Francisco with large quantities of gold as well. Both groups of miners had found their gold in the same place: the Klondike region of northern Canada. Soon these discoveries would make headlines around the world.

4   In a matter of hours, many Seattle residents began planning their own trips to the goldfields. At a time when many Americans were either out of work or earning low wages, the prospect of striking it rich proved irresistible. Firemen, doctors, lawyers, ministers—and even the mayor of Seattle—quit their jobs and joined the rush.

5   "By the afternoon," Pearce wrote, "every man who could raise the necessary funds for a year's **grub stake** was rushing to the grocers, hardware merchants and clothiers to get together the necessary outfit to start by the next boat for the promised land, where the dreams of all should be realized."

• • •

Staking a Claim

6   When **prospectors** found a promising spot, they staked a claim by placing posts at each corner, one with their name and date on it. The prospector then had three days to go to town and file a legal claim. Because the claims were usually measured by **crude** means, disagreements over exact boundaries were common.

7   The first claim in a new location was called the "discovery claim." **Subsequent** claims were legally referred to by their relationship to this claim, along with the name of the creek—5 Above Eldorado, or 6 Below Bonanza, for example.

—Museum at the Klondike Gold Rush National Historical Park, Seattle

. . .

Game of Claim Selling

8   We have received vague rumors about the expected rush here in the spring and we all wonder whether there will be such an enormous crowd as reported. What under the sun they will do is more than any of us can tell. Everything in the country is staked and there certainly won't be employment for all hands, as there is not enough for those here already.

9   Men are busily engaged on schemes to fleece the unsuspecting Cheecakos out of their **tenderfoot** money, and I am afraid many of them will work.

10   Perhaps the name Cheecako is not understood by some in Denver, but it is the Saguache name for greenhorn, or newcomer. We "old-timers" are called "sour doughs," as it is supposed to be part of our education to know how to make sour dough bread.

Typical Klondike Stampede

11   A story of the recent stampede to Swede creek is typical of Dawson life. I was awakened at 1 o'clock in the morning by my partner, Bond, who in a mysterious voice told me to "hurry up, dress and come." "Come where," said I. "Don't say a word but come," said he. "How far?" No answer. "Take any grub?" No answer. So I gave it up and came. Slipping a change of socks and moccasins into my knapsack, together with some hard tack, and belting on my hand ax we started in pitch darkness. We reached Tammany dance hall, where there was an unusual bustle and excitement. I was still half asleep and uncertain whether it was a dream or not. Finally we started up the river. There were about 50 in the party, including four or five dance hall girls. It was inky dark and the river trail has been freshly blown over with snow. We have to go up the river and cross it three times. Soon there was trouble. Men and women were off the

NOTES

trail and up to their necks in snow. Finally some one produced a candle and I volunteered to lead the procession, having had experience carrying a candle underground, I therefore had the **novel** experience of leading a stampede six miles up the Yukon by candle light. Our party of four was one of the first to arrive. We staked by candle light and started home, arriving at Dawson about 9 a.m., having made about 30 miles since 2 o'clock in the morning. Since our staking on Swede creek, in which I got claim number 20, they have staked as high as No. 750 or about 30 miles above my claim, but I haven't yet found out why we went or what caused that stampede.

12. Other stampedes are on very much the same order. This, however, is the only midnight stampede on record. Quite a number regretted going to Swede creek on that trip. At least six men had their feet frozen, and two men died in the hospital from pneumonia. They were careless and did not take proper care of themselves. . .

Stanley H. Pearce

Excerpted from *Call of the Klondike* by David Meissner and Kim Richardson, published by Calkins Creek.

THINK QUESTIONS CA-CCSS: CA.RI.7.1, CA.L.7.4c, CA.L.7.5

1. What did Stanley Pearce and Marshall Bond witness on July 17, 1897? How did Pearce describe the scene? Cite textual evidence to support your answer.

2. What process did prospectors use to stake a claim? Cite specific details from the text.

3. Who describes the stampede to Swede Creek? What role did this person play in the stampede? Why was this stampede unique? Cite textual evidence to support your answer.

4. Use context clues to determine the meaning of **grub stake** as it is used in paragraph 5 of *Call of the Klondike*. Write the definition of the word. Then provide evidence from the paragraph to support your definition of the term, and state whether the word is being used correctly in the excerpt. Consult a print or an online dictionary to find the pronunciation of the word and to verify its part of speech and definition. Examine how the use of "grub stake" has changed over time. Does it have the same meaning now that it had during the time of the Klondike Gold Rush? If not, how might it be used today?

5. Use context clues to determine the meaning of the word **tenderfoot** as it is used in paragraph 9 of *Call of the Klondike*. Write your definition of "tenderfoot." Cite the context clues you used from the text to determine the meaning of the word. Consult a print or an online dictionary to verify its part of speech, definition, and usage. When was the term first used?

Please note that excerpts and passages in the StudySync® library and this workbook are intended as touchstones to generate interest in an author's work. The excerpts and passages do not substitute for the reading of entire texts, and StudySync® strongly recommends that students seek out and purchase the whole literary or informational work in order to experience it as the author intended. Links to online resellers are available in our digital library. In addition, complete works may be ordered through an authorized reseller by filling out and returning to StudySync® the order form enclosed in this workbook.

Reading & Writing Companion

29

CLOSE READ

CA-CCSS: CA.RI.7.1, CA.RI.7.2, CA.RI.7.5a, CA.W.7.2a, CA.W.7.2b, CA.W.7.2d, CA.W.7.5, CA.W.7.6, CA.W.7.10

Reread the excerpt from *Call of the Klondike*. As you reread, complete the Focus Questions below. Then use your answers and annotations from the questions to help you complete the Writing Prompt.

FOCUS QUESTIONS

1. Headings as well as subheads (or subheadings) that appear between paragraphs are one kind of text feature that authors of informational text sometimes use to guide readers through a chapter or a series of chapters. Headings organize the text into smaller sections that help readers locate specific information. Identify the three subheads the authors use in this selection. How do the subheads provide clues to the text structure used throughout the text?

2. Many examples of informational text include features such as sidebars. This is information related to the topic that does not easily fit into the main narrative. It is often set off by bullets or enclosed in a box, separating it from the main text. Which section of text in *Call of the Klondike* serves as a sidebar? How were you able to identify this sidebar? Why is this information separated from the text? What is its purpose?

3. How does the information in the sidebar contribute to the text as a whole, and what does it add to the development of the information in the text? Identify evidence in the text to support your answer.

4. What textual evidence indicates the organizational pattern the authors use to present information under the heading "Typical Klondike Stampede"? Cite text evidence to support your answer.

5. Though there was a lot of gold to be found in the Klondike at the time, striking it rich was not a guarantee. Reread paragraphs 1–5. What drove people to join the gold rush? Highlight textual evidence and make annotations to explain your answer.

WRITING PROMPT

How do the text structure, text features, and added sidebar help you to understand the causes and motivation behind "gold fever" and the process involved in staking a claim? In a clear topic sentence, use these informational text elements (text structure, text features, and sidebar) to make inferences about life in the Klondike, using Pearce's recollection of the stampede to Swede Creek. Organize and support your writing with evidence from the text, using precise language and specific vocabulary choices from the selection.

THE KING OF MAZY MAY

FICTION
Jack London
1899

INTRODUCTION

After gold was discovered in 1896, Jack London was one of the many prospectors who flocked to the Klondike, a remote wilderness area of northwestern Canada, in hopes of striking it rich. Although London never found gold, he came back with a wealth of ideas for his budding career as a writer. Many of London's most popular works, including the short story "The King of Mazy May," were inspired by his experiences during the Klondike Gold Rush.

"He did not dare to think what would happen if they caught him..."

FIRST READ

1   Walt Masters is not a very large boy, but there is manliness in his make-up, and he himself, although he does not know a great deal that most boys know, knows much that other boys do not know. He has never seen a train of cars or an elevator in his life, and for that matter, he has never once looked upon a corn-field, a plow, a cow, or even a chicken. He has never had a pair of shoes on his feet, or gone to a picnic or a party, or talked to a girl. But he has seen the sun at midnight, watched the ice-jams on one of the mightiest of rivers, and played beneath the northern lights, the one white child in thousands of square miles of frozen wilderness.

2   Walt has walked all the fourteen years of his life in sun-tanned, moose-hide moccasins, and he can go to the Indian camps and "talk big" with the men, and trade calico and beads with them for their precious furs. He can make bread without baking-powder, yeast or hops, shoot a moose at three hundred yards, and drive the wild wolf-dogs fifty miles a day on the packed trail.

3   Last of all, he has a good heart, and is not afraid of the darkness and loneliness, of man or beast or thing. His father is a good man, strong and brave, and Walt is growing up like him.

4   Walt was born a thousand miles or so down the Yukon, in a trading-post below the Ramparts. After his mother died, his father and he came on up the river, step by step, from camp to camp, till now they are settled down on the Mazy May Creek in the Klondike country. Last year they and several others had spent much toil and time on the Mazy May, and endured great hardships; the creek, in turn, was just beginning to show up its richness and to reward them for their heavy labor. But with the news of their discoveries, strange men began to come and go through the short days and long nights, and many unjust things they did to the men who had worked so long upon the creek.

5   Si Hartman had gone away on a moose-hunt, to return and find new stakes driven and his claim jumped. George Lukens and his brother had lost their claims in a like manner, having delayed too long on the way to Dawson to record them. In short, it was an old story, and quite a number of the earnest, industrious prospectors had suffered similar losses.

6   But Walt Masters's father had recorded his claim at the start, so Walt had nothing to fear, now that his father had gone on a short trip up the White River prospecting for quartz. Walt was well able to stay by himself in the cabin, cook his three meals a day, and look after things. Not only did he look after his father's claim, but he had agreed to keep an eye on the adjoining one of Loren Hall, who had started for Dawson to record it.

7   Loren Hall was an old man, and he had no dogs, so he had to travel very slowly. After he had been gone some time, word came up the river that he had broken through the ice at Rosebud Creek, and frozen his feet so badly that he would not be able to travel for a couple of weeks. Then Walt Masters received the news that old Loren was nearly all right again, and about to move on afoot for Dawson, as fast as a weakened man could.

8   Walt was worried, however; the claim was liable to be jumped at any moment because of this delay, and a fresh stampede had started in on the Mazy May. He did not like the looks of the newcomers, and one day, when five of them came by with crack dog-teams and the lightest of camping outfits, he could see that they were prepared to make speed, and resolved to keep an eye on them. So he locked up the cabin and followed them, being at the same time careful to remain hidden.

9   He had not watched them long before he was sure that they were professional stampeders, bent on jumping all the claims in sight. Walt crept along the snow at the rim of the creek and saw them change many stakes, destroy old ones, and set up new ones.

10 In the afternoon, with Walt always trailing on their heels, they came back down on the creek, unharnessed their dogs, and went into camp within two claims of his cabin. When he saw them make preparations to cook, he hurried home to get something to eat himself, and then hurried back. He crept so close that he could hear them talking quite plainly, and by pushing the underbrush aside he could catch occasional glimpses of them. They had finished eating and were smoking around the fire.

11 "The creek is all right, boys," a large, black-bearded man, evidently the leader, said, "and I think the best thing we can do is to pull out to-night. The dogs can follow the trail; besides, it's going to be moonlight. What say you?"

NOTES

12 "But it's going to be beastly cold," objected one of the party. "It's forty below zero now."

13 "An' sure, can't ye keep warm by jumpin' on the sleds an' runnin' after the dogs?" cried an Irishman.

14 "An' who wouldn't? The creek as rich as a United States mint! Faith, it's an ilegant chanst to be getting' a run fer yer money! An' if ye don't run, it's mebbe you'll not get the money at all, at all."

15 "That's it," said the leader. "If we can get to Dawson and record, we're rich men; and there is no telling who's been sneaking along in our tracks, watching us, and perhaps now off to give the alarm. The thing for us to do is to rest the dogs a bit, and then hit the trail as hard as we can. What do you say?"

16 Evidently the men had agreed with their leader, for Walt Masters could hear nothing but the rattle of the tin dishes which were being washed. Peering out cautiously, he could see the leader studying a piece of paper. Walt knew what it was at a glance—a list of all the unrecorded claims on Mazy May. Any man could get these lists by applying to the gold commissioner at Dawson.

17 "Thirty-two," the leader said, lifting his face to the men. "Thirty-two isn't recorded, and this is thirty-three. Come on; let's take a look at it. I saw somebody working on it when we came up this morning."

18 Three of the men went with him, leaving one to remain in camp. Walt crept carefully after them till they came to Loren Hall's shaft. One of the men went down and built a fire on the bottom to thaw out the frozen gravel, while the others built another fire on the dump and melted water in a couple of gold-pans. This they poured into a piece of canvas stretched between two logs, used by Loren Hall in which to wash his gold.

19 In a short time a couple of buckets of dirt were sent up by the man in the shaft, and Walt could see the others grouped anxiously about their leader as he proceeded to wash it. When this was finished, they stared at the broad streak of black sand and yellow gold-grains on the bottom of the pan, and one of them called excitedly for the man who had remained in camp to come. Loren Hall had struck it rich, and his claim was not yet recorded. It was plain that they were going to jump it.

20 Walt lay in the snow, thinking rapidly. He was only a boy, but in the face of the threatened injustice against old lame Loren Hall he felt that he must do something. He waited and watched, with his mind made up, till he saw the men began to square up new stakes. Then he crawled away till out of hearing, and broke into a run for the camp of the stampeders. Walt's father had taken their own dogs with him prospecting, and the boy knew how impossible it was for him to undertake the seventy miles to Dawson without the aid of dogs.

21 Gaining the camp, he picked out, with an experienced eye, the easiest running sled and started to harness up the stampeders' dogs. There were three teams of six each, and from there he chose ten of the best. Realizing how necessary it was to have a good head-dog, he strove to discover a leader amongst them; but he had little time in which to do it, for he could hear the voices of the returning men. By the time the team was in shape and everything ready, the claim-jumpers came into sight in an open place not more than a hundred yards from the trail, which ran down the bed of the creek. They cried out to him, but he gave no heed, grabbing up one of their fur sleeping-robes which lay loosely in the snow, and leaping upon the sled.

22 "Mush! Hi! Mush on!" he cried to the animals, snapping the keen-lashed whip among them.

23 The dogs sprang against the yoke-straps, and the sled jerked under way so suddenly as to almost throw him off. Then it curved into the creek, poising perilously on one runner. He was almost breathless with suspense, when it finally righted with a bound and sprang ahead again. The creek bank was high and he could not see, although he could hear the cries of the men and knew they were running to cut him off. He did not dare to think what would happen if they caught him; he only clung to the sled, his heart beating wildly, and watched the snow-rim of the bank above him.

24 Suddenly, over this snow-rim came the flying body of the Irishman, who had leaped straight for the sled in a desperate attempt to capture it; but he was an instant too late. Striking on the very rear of it, he was thrown from his feet, backward, into the snow. Yet, with the quickness of a cat, he had clutched the end of the sled with one hand, turned over, and was dragging behind on his breast, swearing at the boy and threatening all kinds of terrible things if he did not stop the dogs; but Walt cracked him sharply across the knuckles with the butt of the dog-whip till he let go.

25 It was eight miles from Walt's claim to the Yukon—eight very crooked miles, for the creek wound back and forth like a snake, "tying knots in itself," as George Lukens said. And because it was so crooked, the dogs could not get up their best speed, while the sled ground heavily on its side against the curves, now to the right, now to the left.

26 Travellers who had come up and down the Mazy May on foot, with packs on their backs, had declined to go around all the bends, and instead had made short cuts across the narrow necks of creek bottom. Two of his **pursuers** had gone back to harness the remaining dogs, but the others took advantage of these short cuts, running on foot, and before he knew it they had almost overtaken him.

27 "Halt!" they cried after him. "Stop, or we'll shoot!"

28 But Walt only yelled the harder at the dogs, and dashed round the bend with a couple of revolver bullets singing after him. At the next bend they had drawn up closer still, and the bullets struck uncomfortably near to him; but at this point the Mazy May straightened out and ran for half a mile as the crow flies. Here the dogs stretched out in their long wolf-swing, and the stampeders, quickly winded, slowed down and waited for their own sled to come up.

29 Looking over his shoulder, Walt reasoned that they had not given up the chase for good, and that they would soon be after him again. So he wrapped the fur robe about him to shut out the stinging air, and lay flat on the empty sled, encouraging the dogs, as he well knew how.

30 At last, twisting abruptly between two river islands, he came upon the might Yukon sweeping grandly to the north. He could not see from bank to bank, and in the quick-falling twilight it loomed a great white sea of frozen stillness. There was not a sound, save the breathing of the dogs, and the churn of the steel-shod sled.

31 No snow had fallen for several weeks, and the traffic had packed the main-river trail till it was hard and glassy as glare ice. Over this the sled flew along, and the dogs kept the trail fairly well, although Walt quickly discovered that he had made a mistake in choosing the leader. As they were driven in single file, without reins, he had to guide them by his voice, and it was evident that the head-dog had never learned the meaning of "gee" and "haw." He hugged the inside of the curves too closely, often forcing his comrades behind him into the soft snow, while several times he thus **capsized** the sled.

32 There was no wind, but the speed at which he travelled created a bitter blast, and with the thermometer down to forty below, this bit through fur and flesh to the very bones. Aware that if he remained constantly upon the sled he would freeze to death, and knowing the practice of Arctic travellers, Walt shortened up one of the lashing-thongs, and whenever he felt chilled, seized hold of it, jumped off, and ran behind till warmth was restored. Then he would climb on and rest till the process had to be repeated.

33 Looking back he could see the sled of his pursuers, drawn by eight dogs, rising and falling over the ice **hummocks** like a boat in a seaway. The Irishman and the black-bearded leader were with it, taking turns in running and riding.

34 Night fell, and in the blackness of the first hour or so, Walt toiled desperately with his dogs. On account of the poor lead-dog, they were constantly **floundering** off the beaten track into the soft snow, and the sled was as often riding on its side or top as it was in the proper way. This work and strain tried his strength sorely. Had he not been in such haste he could have avoided much of it, but he feared the stampeders would creep up in the darkness and

overtake him. However, he could hear them occasionally yelling to their dogs, and knew from the sounds that they were coming up very slowly.

35   When the moon rose he was off Sixty Mile, and Dawson was only fifty miles away. He was almost exhausted, and breathed a sigh of relief as he climbed on the sled again. Looking back, he saw his enemies had crawled up within four hundred yards. At this space they remained, a black speck of motion on the white river-beast. Strive as they would, they could not shorten this distance, and strive as he would he could not increase it.

36   He had now discovered the proper lead-dog, and he knew he could easily run away from them if he could only change the bad leader for the good one. But this was impossible, for a moment's delay, at the speed they were running, would bring the men behind upon him.

37   When he got off the mouth of Rosebud Creek, just as he was topping a rise, the ping of a bullet on the ice beside him, and the report of a gun, told him that they were this time shooting at him with a rifle. And from then on, as he cleared the summit of each ice-jam, he stretched flat on the leaping sled till the rifle-shot from the rear warned him that he was safe till the next ice-jam.

38   Now it is very hard to lie on a moving sled, jumping and plunging and yawing like a boat before the wind, and to shoot through the deceiving moonlight at an object four hundred yards away on another moving sled performing equally wild antics. So it is not to be wondered at that the black-bearded leader did not hit him.

39   After several hours of this, during which, perhaps, a score of bullets had struck about him, their ammunition began to give out and their fire slackened. They took greater care, and only whipped a shot at him at the most favorable opportunities. He was also beginning to leave them behind, the distance slowly increasing to six hundred yards.

40   Lifting clear on the crest of a great jam off Indian River, Walt Masters met his first accident. A bullet sang past his ears, and struck the bad lead-dog.

41   The poor brute plunged in a heap, with the rest of the team on top of him.

42   Like a flash, Walt was by the leader. Cutting the **traces** with his hunting knife, he dragged the dying animal to one side and straightened out the team.

43   He glanced back. The other sled was coming up like an express-train. With half the dogs still over their traces, he cried, "Mush on!" and leaped upon the sled just as the pursuing team dashed abreast of him.

NOTES

44 The Irishman was just preparing to spring for him,—they were so sure they had him that they did not shoot,—when Walt turned fiercely upon them with his whip.

45 He struck at their faces, and men must save their faces with their hands. So there was not shooting just then. Before they could recover from the hot rain of blows, Walt reached out from his sled, catching their wheel-dog by the fore legs in midspring, and throwing him heavily. This brought the whole team into a snarl, capsizing the sled and tangling his enemies up beautifully.

46 Away Walt flew, the runners of his sled fairly screaming as they bounded over the frozen surface. And what had seemed an accident, proved to be a blessing in disguise. The proper lead-dog was now to the fore, and he stretched low to the trail and whined with joy as he jerked his comrades along.

47 By the time he reached Ainslie's Creek, seventeen miles from Dawson, Walt had left his pursuers, a tiny speck, far behind. At Monte Cristo Island, he could no longer see them. And at Swede Creek, just as daylight was silvering the pines, he ran plump into the camp of old Loren Hall.

48 Almost as quick as it takes to tell it, Loren had his sleeping-furs rolled up, and had joined Walt on the sled. They permitted the dogs to travel more slowly, as there was no sign of the chase in the rear, and just as they pulled up at the gold commissioner's office in Dawson, Walt, who had kept his eyes open to the last, fell asleep.

49 And because of what Walt Masters did on this night, the men of the Yukon have become very proud of him, and always speak of him now as the King of Mazy May.

THINK QUESTIONS CA-CCSS: CA.RL.7.1, CA.L.7.4a

1. How is Walt different from most boys? Cite specific textual evidence to support your answer.

2. How do Walt's efforts to help Loren Hall lead to conflict in the story? Find specific evidence in the text to support your answer.

3. Why do the men of the Yukon call Walt "the King of Mazy May"? Refer to specific details in the text to support your answer.

4. Use context clues to determine the meaning of the word **capsized** as it is used in paragraph 31

of the text. Write your definition of "capsized" and cite the context clues that helped you figure out the meaning of the word.

5. Find the sentence in paragraph 33 that contains the word **hummocks**. Use context clues to determine the meaning of the word. Then use a print or an online dictionary to confirm the meaning as it is used in *The King of Mazy May*. Revise your definition as needed.

CLOSE READ

CA-CCSS: CA.RL.7.1, CA.RL.7.2, CA.RL.7.3, CA.RL.7.9, CA.W.7.2a, CA.W.7.2b, CA.W.7.2d, CA.W.7.2f, CA.W.7.4, CA.W.7.5, CA.W.7.6, CA.W.7.9a, CA.W.7.10

Reread the short story "The King of Mazy May." As you reread, complete the Focus Questions below. Then use your answers and annotations from the questions to help you complete the Writing Prompt.

 FOCUS QUESTIONS

1. Reread this sentence in paragraph 9 of *Call of the Klondike*: "Men are busily engaged on schemes to fleece the unsuspecting Cheecakos out of their tenderfoot money, and I am afraid many of them will work." How does Jack London use these historical facts in paragraph 4 of "The King of Mazy May"? How does he change them? Highlight textual evidence and make annotations to explain your response.

2. In paragraph 8 of "The King of Mazy May," what inference can you make about the newcomers based on specific details in the text? Highlight textual evidence and make annotations to explain your choice.

3. In paragraphs 25 and 26 in "The King of Mazy May," how does the setting affect the plot? Highlight textual evidence and make annotations to support your ideas.

4. Compare and contrast the dangerous conditions posed by the cold as they are described in *Call of the Klondike* and "The King of Mazy May." Based on the historical account in *Call of the Klondike,* how accurately does the short story portray the effects of the frozen terrain on the people living there? Highlight textual evidence and make annotations to explain your choices.

5. In "The King of Mazy May," what motivates Walt to go to extreme lengths to protect Loren Hall's claim? What inferences can you make about Walt's character from his decision to undertake the mission to help Loren Hall? Highlight textual evidence that supports your inferences, and make annotations to cite some of Walt's character traits that affect the setting, characters, plot, and theme of the story.

WRITING PROMPT

Jack London was famous for portraying history accurately in his short stories. What inferences can you make about the Klondike Gold Rush from reading "The King of Mazy May"? What textual evidence in *Call of the Klondike*, a historical account of the Klondike Gold Rush, supports or refutes the idea that London portrayed history accurately in his short story? Begin your response to the prompt with a clear statement that explains your topic. Organize and support your writing with specific evidence, using precise language and selection vocabulary from the factual *Call of the Klondike* and from London's fictional story "The King of Mazy May." Conclude with a statement that supports your main ideas.

Please note that excerpts and passages in the StudySync® library and this workbook are intended as touchstones to generate interest in an author's work. The excerpts and passages do not substitute for the reading of entire texts, and StudySync® strongly recommends that students seek out and purchase the whole literary or informational work in order to experience it as the author intended. Links to online resellers are available in our digital library. In addition, complete works may be ordered through an authorized reseller by filling out and returning to StudySync® the order form enclosed in this workbook.

Reading & Writing Companion

39

THE CREMATION OF SAM MCGEE

POETRY
Robert W. Service
1907

INTRODUCTION

Originally published in 1907 in the poetry collection *Songs of a Sourdough*, "The Cremation of Sam McGee" was the most popular of Robert Service's many poems. This entertaining and colorful piece paints a vibrant picture of the characters and setting of the Klondike Gold Rush in Canada and Alaska at the end of the 19th Century. Service was an eyewitness to the end of this dynamic period of North American history, as the last great sweep of gold fever played out in the grandeur of the untamed West.

"The trail was bad, and I felt half mad, but I swore I would not give in..."

FIRST READ

NOTES

1 *There are strange things done in the midnight sun*
2 *By the men who moil for gold;*
3 *The Arctic trails have their secret tales*
4 *That would make your blood run cold;*
5 *The Northern Lights have seen queer sights,*
6 *But the queerest they ever did see*
7 *Was that night on the marge of Lake Lebarge*
8 *I cremated Sam McGee.*

9 Now Sam McGee was from Tennessee, where the cotton blooms and blows.
10 Why he left his home in the South to roam 'round the Pole, God only knows.
11 He was always cold, but the land of gold seemed to hold him like a spell;
12 Though he'd often say in his homely way that "he'd sooner live in hell."

13 On a Christmas Day we were mushing our way over the Dawson trail.
14 Talk of your cold! through the parka's fold it stabbed like a driven nail.
15 If our eyes we'd close, then the lashes froze till sometimes we couldn't see;
16 It wasn't much fun, but the only one to whimper was Sam McGee.

17 And that very night, as we lay packed tight in our robes beneath the snow,
18 And the dogs were fed, and the stars o'erhead were dancing heel and toe,
19 He turned to me, and "Cap," says he, "I'll cash in this trip, I guess;
20 And if I do, I'm asking that you won't refuse my last request."

21 Well, he seemed so low that I couldn't say no; then he says with a sort of moan:
22 "It's the cursed cold, and it's got right hold till I'm chilled clean through to the bone.
23 Yet 'taint being dead—it's my awful dread of the icy grave that pains;
24 So I want you to swear that, foul or fair, you'll cremate my last remains."

Please note that excerpts and passages in the StudySync® library and this workbook are intended as touchstones to generate interest in an author's work. The excerpts and passages do not substitute for the reading of entire texts, and StudySync® strongly recommends that students seek out and purchase the whole literary or informational work in order to experience it as the author intended. Links to online resellers are available in our digital library. In addition, complete works may be ordered through an authorized reseller by filling out and returning to StudySync® the order form enclosed in this workbook.

Reading & Writing Companion **41**

NOTES

25 A pal's last need is a thing to **heed**, so I swore I would not fail;
26 And we started on at the streak of dawn; but God! he looked **ghastly** pale.
27 He crouched on the sleigh, and he raved all day of his home in Tennessee;
28 And before nightfall a corpse was all that was left of Sam McGee.

29 There wasn't a breath in that land of death, and I hurried, horror-driven,
30 With a corpse half hid that I couldn't get rid, because of a promise given;
31 It was lashed to the sleigh, and it seemed to say: "You may tax your brawn and brains,
32 But you promised true, and it's up to you to cremate those last remains."

33 Now a promise made is a debt unpaid, and the trail has its own stern code.
34 In the days to come, though my lips were dumb, in my heart how I cursed that load.
35 In the long, long night, by the lone firelight, while the huskies, round in a ring,
36 Howled out their woes to the homeless snows—O God! how I **loathed** the thing.

37 And every day that quiet clay seemed to heavy and heavier grow;
38 And on I went, though the dogs were spent and the grub was getting low;
39 The trail was bad, and I felt half mad, but I swore I would not give in;
40 And I'd often sing to the hateful thing, and it hearkened with a grin.

41 Till I came to the marge of Lake Lebarge, and a derelict there lay;
42 It was jammed in the ice, but I saw in a trice it was called the "Alice May."
43 And I looked at it, and I thought a bit, and I looked at my frozen chum;
44 Then "Here," said I, with a sudden cry, "is my cre-ma-tor-eum."

45 Some planks I tore from the cabin floor, and I lit the boiler fire;
46 Some coal I found that was lying around, and I heaped the fuel higher;
47 The flames just soared and the furnace roared—such a blaze you seldom see;
48 Then I burrowed a hole in the glowing coal, and I stuffed in Sam McGee.

49 Then I made a hike, for I didn't like to hear him sizzle so;
50 And the heavens **scowled,** and the huskies howled, and the wind began to blow.
51 It was icy cold, but the hot sweat rolled down my cheeks, and I don't know why;
52 And the greasy smoke in an inky cloak went streaking down the sky.

53 I do not know how long in the snow I wrestled with **grisly** fear;
54 But the stars came out and they danced about ere again I ventured near;
55 I was sick with dread, but I bravely said: "I'll just take a peep inside.
56 I guess he's cooked, and it's time I looked;" . . . then the door I opened wide.

NOTES

57 And there sat Sam, looking cool and calm, in the heart of the furnace roar;

58 And he wore a smile you could see a mile, and he said: "Please close that door.

59 It's fine in here, but I greatly fear you'll let in the cold and storm—

60 Since I left Plumtree, down in Tennessee, it's the first time I've been warm."

61 *There are strange things done in the midnight sun*

62 *By the men who moil for gold;*

63 *The Arctic trails have their secret tales*

64 *That would make your blood run cold;*

65 *The Northern Lights have seen queer sights,*

66 *But the queerest they ever did see*

67 *Was that night on the marge of Lake Lebarge*

68 *I cremated Sam McGee.*

THINK QUESTIONS   CA-CCSS: CA.RL.7.1, CA.L.7.4a, CA.L.7.4c, CA.L.7.5b, CA.SL.7.1a, CA.SL.7.1c, CA.SL.7.1d, CA.SL.7.3

1. Which details in the poem provide evidence that it is set during the Klondike Gold Rush in Canada and Alaska? Cite at least three specific examples from the text.

2. What is Sam McGee most afraid of? What does he ask his friend Cap to do because of this fear? Cite specific details and figurative language from the poem to support your answer.

3. This poem has a surprise ending. Use textual evidence to describe the unexpected event at the end of the poem. How does this unexpected twist add to the humor in the poem?

4. The word **cremate** appears in different forms in the poem: "cremation," "cremate," "cremated," and "crematorium." What does it mean to cremate someone? Use context clues in the poem to determine the meaning of the word. Write your definition of "cremate" and tell how you figured out the meaning. Cite specific evidence from the text.

5. Use a print or digital dictionary to determine the meaning of the word **grisly** as it is used in line 53 of stanza 13. Then find synonyms of the word in a print or digital thesaurus. Write your definition and synonyms and tell where you found them.

Please note that excerpts and passages in the StudySync® library and this workbook are intended as touchstones to generate interest in an author's work. The excerpts and passages do not substitute for the reading of entire texts, and StudySync® strongly recommends that students seek out and purchase the whole literary or informational work in order to experience it as the author intended. Links to online resellers are available in our digital library. In addition, complete works may be ordered through an authorized reseller by filling out and returning to StudySync® the order form enclosed in this workbook.

Reading & Writing Companion   **43**

CLOSE READ

CA-CCSS: CA.RL.7.1, CA.RL.7.2, CA.RL.7.4, CA.RL.7.5, CA.W.7.2a, CA.W.7.2b, CA.W.7.2d, CA.W.7.4, CA.W.7.5, CA.W.7.6, CA.W.7.10, CA.L.7.4a

Reread the poem "I Cremated Sam McGee." As you reread, complete the Focus Questions below. Then use your answers and annotations from the questions to help you complete the Writing Prompt.

FOCUS QUESTIONS

1. Highlight the rhyme within lines and at the ends of lines in stanza 3, beginning with "On a Christmas Day." Then imagine that the poet had written this 4-line stanza without using rhyme. Would this simple verse be more or less effective without rhyme? How might it sound like a story? Support your opinion with specific evidence from the text.

2. Highlight two examples of personification in stanza 12. What does the personification help you to visualize? Cite specific evidence from the text.

3. Stanza 14 includes a poetic element that is often found in tall tales—hyperbole. Hyperbole is a poetic device that uses exaggeration to express emotion or surprise, make a point, or create

humor. Highlight the hyperbole in the stanza. How does it help create humor in the poem? Cite specific evidence from the text.

4. Summarize the poetic structure used in "The Cremation of Sam McGee." Include the form of the poem in your written summary, the use of stanzas, rhyme scheme (pattern of end rhymes), refrain (or repeated stanza), and an inference about why the ballad form was likely used. Highlight specific evidence from the text and make annotations to record notes for your objective summary of the poem's structure.

5. What can the reader infer is the speaker's motivation for undertaking the mission of fulfilling Sam McGee's last wish? Highlight textual evidence to support your answer.

WRITING PROMPT

"The Cremation of Sam McGee" is a study in contrasts. It includes language and imagery that point to the grim nature of death, and yet it also makes readers laugh about this serious subject. How does the poem use poetic structure and form, as well as poetic elements like rhyme, figurative language and imagery, and tone, to produce this contrast? Begin with a statement that clearly explains your topic. Organize and support your writing with specific evidence from the text. Pay careful attention to your word choice, and use precise language and vocabulary from the selection.

NEW DIRECTIONS

NON-FICTION
Maya Angelou
1993

INTRODUCTION

"New Directions" is Maya Angelou's biographical essay about her grandmother, Annie Johnson. When Annie's marriage ends in 1903, she realizes that she must work in order to support her two small boys. As an African-American woman, her choices are limited, yet Annie "cuts a new path" for herself through hard work and resourcefulness. In sharing her grandmother's story, Angelou teaches readers a lesson about the importance of making deliberate choices.

"I decided to step off the road and cut me a new path."

FIRST READ

1   In 1903 the late Mrs. Annie Johnson of Arkansas found herself with two toddling sons, very little money, a slight ability to read and add simple numbers. To this picture add a disastrous marriage and the burdensome fact that Mrs. Johnson was a Negro.

2   When she told her husband, Mr. William Johnson, of her dissatisfaction with their marriage, he **conceded** that he too found it to be less than he expected, and had been secretly hoping to leave and study religion. He added that he thought God was calling him not only to preach but to do so in Enid, Oklahoma. He did not tell her that he knew a minister in Enid with whom he could study and who had a friendly, unmarried daughter. They parted amicably, Annie keeping the one-room house and William taking most of the cash to carry himself to Oklahoma.

3   Annie, over six feet tall, big-boned, decided that she would not go to work as a **domestic** and leave her "precious babes" to anyone else's care. There was no possibility of being hired at the town's cotton gin or lumber mill, but maybe there was a way to make the two factories work for her. In her words, "I looked up the road I was going and back the way I come, and since I wasn't satisfied, I decided to step off the road and cut me a new path." She told herself that she wasn't a fancy cook but that she could "mix groceries well enough to scare hungry away and from starving a man."

4   She made her plans **meticulously** and in secret. One early evening to see if she was ready, she placed stones in two five-gallon pails and carried them three miles to the cotton gin. She rested a little, and then, discarding some rocks, she walked in the darkness to the saw mill five miles farther along the dirt road. On her way back to her little house and her babies, she dumped the remaining rocks along the path.

5   That same night she worked into the early hours boiling chicken and frying ham. She made dough and filled the rolled-out pastry with meat. At last she went to sleep.

6   The next morning she left her house carrying the meat pies, lard, an iron brazier, and coals for a fire. Just before lunch she appeared in an empty lot behind the cotton gin. As the dinner noon bell rang, she dropped the savors into boiling fat and the aroma rose and floated over to the workers who spilled out of the gin, covered with white lint, looking like specters.

7   Most workers had brought their lunches of pinto beans and biscuits or crackers, onions and cans of sardines, but they were tempted by the hot meat pies which Annie ladled out of the fat. She wrapped them in newspapers, which soaked up the grease, and offered them for sale at a nickel each. Although business was slow, those first days Annie was determined. She balanced her appearances between the two hours of activity.

8   So, on Monday if she offered hot fresh pies at the cotton gin and sold the remaining cooled-down pies at the lumber mill for three cents, then on Tuesday she went first to the lumber mill presenting fresh, just-cooked pies as the lumbermen covered in sawdust emerged from the mill.

9   For the next few years, on balmy spring days, blistering summer noon, and cold, wet, and wintry middays, Annie never disappointed her customers, who could count on seeing the tall, brown-skin woman bent over her brazier, carefully turning the meat pies. When she felt certain that the workers had become dependent on her, she built a stall between the two hives of industry and let the men run to her for their lunchtime provisions.

10 She had indeed stepped from the road which seemed to have been chosen for her and cut herself a brand-new path. In years that stall became a store where customers could buy cheese, meal, syrup, cookies, candy, writing tablets, pickles, canned goods, fresh fruit, soft drinks, coal oil, and leather soles for worn-out shoes.

11 Each of us has the right and the responsibility to **assess** the roads which lie ahead, and those over which we have traveled, and if the future road looms **ominous** or unpromising, and the roads back uninviting, then we need to gather our resolve and, carrying only the necessary baggage, step off that road into another direction. If the new choice is also unpalatable, without embarrassment, we must be ready to change that as well.

"New Directions" from WOULDN'T TAKE NOTHING FOR MY JOURNEY NOW by Maya Angelou, copyright © 1993 by Maya Angelou. Used by permission of Random House, an imprint and division of Random House LLC. All rights reserved.

THINK QUESTIONS GA-CCSS: CA.RI.7.1, CA.L.7.4a, CA.L.7.5c

1. Why did Annie Johnson need to find a way to make money? What information in the text tells you this? Cite specific textual evidence to support your answer.

2. What did Annie decide to do to make money? How do you know? Cite specific evidence from the text to support your answer.

3. What was the final outcome of Annie's decision to sell food to the workers in order to support her family? What clues helped you infer this? Cite specific textual evidence to support your inference.

4. What is the denotation, or dictionary definition, of the word **conceded** as it is used in paragraph 2?

What is its connotation in the text? Use context to describe the word's connotation in "New Directions." Cite specific evidence from the text to support your answer.

5. What is the definition of **meticulously** as it is used in paragraph 4? By remembering that the suffix -*ly* means "in a certain way," use that information, along with context clues provided in the passage, to determine the meaning of "meticulously." Write your definition of the word and tell how you figured out its meaning. Cite specific evidence from the text to support your answer.

CLOSE READ

CA-CCSS: CA.RI.7.1, CA.RI.7.2, CA.RI.7.3, CA.RI.7.4, CA.RI.7.5, CA.L.7.4c, CA.L.7.5a, CA.L.7.5c, CA.W.7.2a, CA.W.7.2b, CA.W.7.2d, CA.W.7.2f, CA.W.7.4, CA.W.7.5, CA.W.7.6, CA.W.7.10

Reread the essay "New Directions." As you reread, complete the Focus Questions below. Then use your answers and annotations from the questions to help you complete the Writing Prompt.

FOCUS QUESTIONS

1. As you reread the text of "New Directions," look for interactions among the individuals, events, and ideas to get a deeper understanding of the text. For example, in what ways did Annie's dissatisfaction with her marriage change her life? Highlight evidence in the text and make annotations to support your choices.

2. Connotation helps an author convey meaning. Why does Maya Angelou choose to use the word "meticulously" in paragraph 4, rather than "carefully"? Look in a dictionary for the exact meaning of "meticulous." What is the impact of this specific word choice on the meaning of the text? What does the word connote about Annie's personality? Highlight specific textual evidence and make annotations to support your response.

3. An author may use the same metaphor comparing two unlike things throughout a text. This is called an extended metaphor. In "New Directions," the metaphor of life as a road is an extended metaphor. After Annie herself is quoted in paragraph 3 as comparing her life to a road,

where else does the metaphor appear in the text? How does the author use this extended metaphor to convey a central idea? Highlight textual evidence and make annotations to support your response.

4. Connotation adds depth to a text and makes reading a richer experience. Use your understanding of denotation and connotation to explain why Maya Angelou used the term "big-boned" rather than just "large" to describe Annie, and "savors" rather than just "food" to describe the pies she made. Highlight specific evidence in the text and make annotations to support your choices.

5. If you think about how ideas and events affect individuals, you might be able to explain why people act the way they do. Make an inference about what drove Annie to walk with pails of rocks to the factories. How did this action confirm her mission to find a "new direction" in life? Highlight evidence in the text and make annotations to explain your response.

WRITING PROMPT

Why does Maya Angelou use the extended metaphor that compares life to a road? What does the metaphor mean in the text? What is its purpose? Begin with a clear statement of explanation. How does this extended metaphor develop the central idea of this biographical excerpt? Organize and support your writing with specific evidence from the text. Use precise language and vocabulary from the selection. Provide a strong conclusion that supports your main ideas.

Please note that excerpts and passages in the StudySync® library and this workbook are intended as touchstones to generate interest in an author's work. The excerpts and passages do not substitute for the reading of entire texts, and StudySync® strongly recommends that students seek out and purchase the whole literary or informational work in order to experience it as the author intended. Links to online resellers are available in our digital library. In addition, complete works may be ordered through an authorized reseller by filling out and returning to StudySync® the order form enclosed in this workbook.   Reading & Writing Companion   **49**

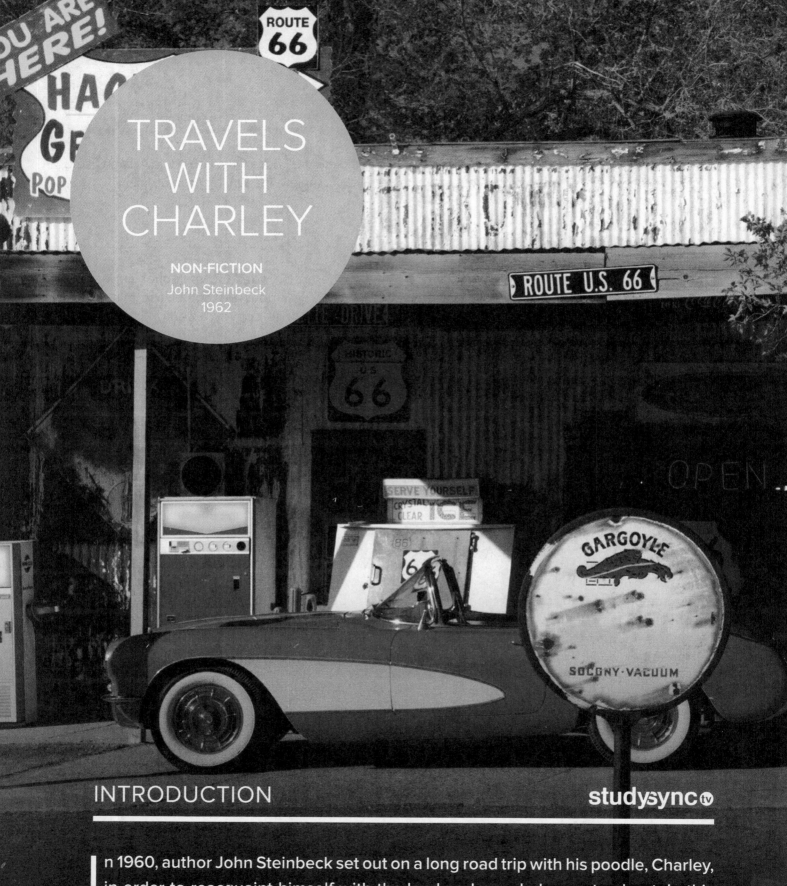

TRAVELS WITH CHARLEY

NON-FICTION
John Steinbeck
1962

INTRODUCTION

studysync tv

n 1960, author John Steinbeck set out on a long road trip with his poodle, Charley, in order to reacquaint himself with the land and people he wrote about. In this excerpt from his Pulitzer Prize winning book about the experience, he shares various observations.

"For how can one know color in perpetual green?"

 FIRST READ

1 I soon discovered that if a wayfaring stranger wishes to eavesdrop on a local population, the places for him to slip in and hold his peace are bars and churches. But some New England towns don't have bars, and church is only on Sunday. A good **alternative** is the roadside restaurant where men gather for breakfast before going to work or going hunting. To find these places inhabited one must get up very early. And there is a drawback even to this. Early-rising men not only do not talk much to strangers, they barely talk to one another. Breakfast conversation is limited to a series of laconic grunts. The natural New England taciturnity reaches its glorious perfection at breakfast.

2 I fed Charley, gave him a limited **promenade**, and hit the road. An icy mist covered the hills and froze on my windshield. I am not normally a breakfast eater, but here I had to be or I wouldn't see anybody unless I stopped for gas. At the first lighted roadside restaurant I pulled in and took my seat at a counter. The customers were folded over their coffee cups like ferns. A normal conversation is as follows:

3 WAITRESS: "Same?"

4 CUSTOMER: "Yep."

5 WAITRESS: "Cold enough for you?"

6 CUSTOMER: "Yep."

7 WAITRESS: "Refill?"

8 CUSTOMER: "Yep."

9 This is a really talkative customer. Some reduce it to "Burp" and others do not answer at all. An early morning waitress in New England leads a lonely life,

but I soon learned that if I tried to **inject** life and gaiety into her job with a blithe remark she dropped her eyes and answered "Yep" or "Umph." Still, I did feel that there was some kind of communication, but I can't say what it was.

10 The best of learning came on the morning radio, which I learned to love. Every town of a few thousand people has its station, and it takes the place of the old local newspaper. Bargains and trades are announced, social doings, prices of commodities, messages. The records played are the same all over the country. If "Teen-Age Angel" is top of the list in Maine, it is top of the list in Montana. In the course of a day you may hear "Teen-Age Angel" thirty or forty times. But in addition to local news and **chronicles,** some foreign advertising creeps in. As I went farther and farther north and it got colder I was aware of more and more advertising for Florida real estate and, with the approach of the long and bitter winter, I could see why Florida is a golden word. As I went along I found that more and more people lusted toward Florida and that thousands had moved there and more thousands wanted to and would. The advertising, with a side look at Federal Communications, made few claims except for the fact that the land they were selling was in Florida. Some of them went out on a limb and promised that it was above tide level. But that didn't matter; the very name Florida carried the message of warmth and ease and comfort. It was irresistible.

11 I've lived in good climate, and it bores the hell out of me. I like weather rather than climate. In Cuernavaca, Mexico, where I once lived, and where the climate is as near to perfect as is conceivable, I have found that when people leave there they usually go to Alaska. I'd like to see how long an Aroostook County man can stand Florida.

12 The trouble is that with his savings moved and invested there, he can't very well go back. His dice are rolled and can't be picked up again. But I do wonder if a down-Easter, sitting on a nylon-and-aluminum chair out on a changelessly green lawn slapping mosquitoes in the evening of a Florida October—I do wonder if the stab of memory doesn't strike him high in the stomach just below the ribs where it hurts. And in the humid ever-summer I dare his picturing mind not to go back to the shout of color, to the clean rasp of frosty air, to the smell of pine wood burning and the caressing warmth of kitchens. For how can one know color in perpetual green, and what good is warmth without cold to give it sweetness?

13 I drove as slowly as custom and the impatient law permitted. That's the only way to see anything. Every few miles the states provided places of rest off the roads, sheltered places sometimes near dark streams. There were painted oil drums for garbage, and picnic tables, and sometimes fireplaces or barbecue pits. At **intervals** I drove Rocinante off the road and let Charley out to smell over the register of previous guests. Then I would heat my coffee

NOTES

and sit comfortably on my back step and contemplate wood and water and the quick-rising mountains with crowns of conifers and the fir trees high up, dusted with snow. Long ago at Easter I had a looking-egg. Peering in a little porthole at the end, I saw a lovely little farm, a kind of dream farm, and on the farmhouse chimney a stork sitting on a nest. I regarded this as a fairy-tale farm as surely imagined as gnomes sitting under toadstools. And then in Denmark I saw that farm or its brother, and it was true, just as it had been in the looking-egg. And in Salinas, California, where I grew up, although we had some frost the climate was cool and foggy. When we saw colored pictures of a Vermont autumn forest it was another fairy thing and we frankly didn't believe it. In school we memorized "Snowbound" and little poems about Old Jack Frost and his paintbrush, but the only thing Jack Frost did for us was put a thin skin of ice on the watering trough, and that rarely. To find not only that this bedlam of color was true but that the pictures were pale and inaccurate translations, was to me startling. I can't even imagine the forest colors when I am not seeing them. I wondered whether constant association could cause inattention, and asked a native New Hampshire woman about it. She said the autumn never failed to amaze her; to elate. "It is a glory," she said, "and can't be remembered, so that it always comes as a surprise."

Excerpted from *Travels with Charley* by John Steinbeck, published by the Penguin Group.

THINK QUESTIONS   CA-CCSS: CA.RI.7.1, CA.L.7.4a, CA.L.7.4b, CA.SL.7.1a, CA.SL.7.1b, CA.SL.7.1c, CA.SL.7.1d, CA.SL.7.2

1. About how long ago do you think this selection was written? Highlight textual evidence and make annotations to identify details that reveal the time period.

2. Why does listening to the radio give the author a better idea of what people are thinking than visiting local roadside restaurants? Cite textual evidence to support your answer.

3. What does Steinbeck love about the weather in New England? Refer to evidence in the text to support your answer.

4. Use context to determine the meaning of the word **alternative** as it is used in the first paragraph of *Travels with Charley*. Write your definition of "alternative" and tell how you figured out its meaning.

5. By remembering that the Latin prefix *inter-* means "between," use the context clues provided in the passage to determine the meaning of **intervals,** in paragraph 13. Write your definition and tell how you determined the meaning of the word.

CLOSE READ

CA-CCSS: CA.RI.7.1, CA.RI.7.2, CA.RI.7.3, CA.L.7.5a, CA.L.7.5c, CA.W.7.2a, CA.W.7.2b, CA.W.7.2d, CA.W.7.2f, CA.W.7.4, CA.W.7.5, CA.W.7.6, CA.W.7.10

Reread the excerpt from *Travels With Charley*. As you reread, complete the Focus Questions below. Then use your answers and annotations from the questions to help you complete the Writing Prompt.

FOCUS QUESTIONS

1. In *Travels with Charley*, John Steinbeck is driven to undertake a mission. During his mission—a cross-country road trip—readers come to understand that the interactions between an event, individuals, and the idea that springs from these interactions all influence one another. What did Steinbeck's interactions with New Englanders reveal about them, and what conclusions did the author reach as a result? Highlight textual evidence to support your answer.

2. What conclusions was Steinbeck able to draw about small-town life by listening to local morning radio shows? Annotate to explain how these details help develop the ideas and advance the events in the selection.

3. An author of informational text will sometimes use figurative language to persuade readers to share a point of view, or to enhance an argument. In the second half of the excerpt, Steinbeck includes descriptive details that help bring his perceptions and opinions to life. Annotate examples in the text where Steinbeck uses figurative language to underscore how he feels about Florida.

4. Why does Steinbeck describe the looking-egg he used to have? What central idea in the text does it help you understand? Look for textual evidence that supports your answer.

5. In the last paragraph, Steinbeck has a conversation with a New Hampshire woman about the colors of the forest in autumn. What does he learn from this conversation? How might it reaffirm his earlier idea that a New Englander might have regrets about moving to Florida? Support your statements with textual evidence.

WRITING PROMPT

What insights, or new ideas, has John Steinbeck gained from his decision to travel with his dog, Charley, through New England? Does he seem to be succeeding in his mission to "reacquaint himself with the land and the people he wrote about"? How are the people influencing his ideas about New England and his experiences there? Begin your writing with a clear sentence explaining your topic. Organize and support your ideas in a well-written paragraph that cites specific evidence from the text. Use precise language and vocabulary from the selection. Complete your writing with a concluding statement that summarizes your central ideas.

APOLLO 13: MISSION HIGHLIGHTS

NON-FICTION
NASA Kennedy Space Center
1970

INTRODUCTION

Their mission was to be an exploration of a lunar highland, following after the successful landings of *Apollo 11 and 12*. However, *Apollo 13* would prove unlucky. Nearing the moon, both oxygen tanks in the command module (CM) failed, shutting down power and forcing the crew to abandon the mission and focus on getting home safely—while crammed into the smaller lunar module (LM).

"Houston, we've had a problem here."

 FIRST READ

Mission Highlights

1   The first two days the crew ran into a couple of minor surprises, but generally *Apollo 13* was looking like the smoothest flight of the program. At 46 hours 43 minutes Joe Kerwin, the CapCom on duty, said, "The spacecraft is in real good shape as far as we are concerned. We're bored to tears down here." It was the last time anyone would mention boredom for a long time.

2   At 55 hours 46 minutes, as the crew finished a 49-minute TV broadcast showing how comfortably they lived and worked in weightlessness, Lovell stated: "This is the crew of *Apollo 13* wishing everybody there a nice evening, and we're just about ready to close out our inspection of *Aquarius (the LM)* and get back for a pleasant evening in *Odyssey (the CM)*. Good night."

3   Nine minutes later, Oxygen tank No. 2 blew up, causing No. 1 tank also to fail. *The Apollo 13* command module's normal supply of electricity, light, and water was lost, and they were about 200,000 miles from Earth.

4   The message came in the form of a sharp bang and vibration. Jack Swigert saw a warning light that accompanied the bang, and said, "Houston, we've had a problem here." Lovell came on and told the ground that it was a main B bus undervolt. The time was 2108 hours on April 13.

5   Next, the warning lights indicated the loss of two of *Apollo 13's* three fuel cells, which were the spacecraft's prime source of electricity. With warning lights blinking on, one oxygen tank appeared to be completely empty, and there were indications that the oxygen in the second tank was rapidly being **depleted.**

6   Thirteen minutes after the explosion, Lovell happened to look out of the left-hand window, and saw the final evidence pointing toward **potential**

catastrophe. "We are venting something out into the- into space," he reported to Houston. Jack Lousma, the CapCom replied, "Roger, we copy you venting." Lovell said, "It's a gas of some sort." It was oxygen gas escaping at a high rate from the second, and last, oxygen tank.

7   The first thing the crew did, even before discovering the oxygen leak, was to try to close the hatch between the CM and the LM. They reacted spontaneously, like submarine crews, closing the hatches to limit the amount of flooding. First Jack and then Lovell tried to lock the reluctant hatch, but the stubborn lid wouldn't stay shut. Exasperated, and realizing that there wasn't a cabin leak, they strapped the hatch to the CM couch.

8   The pressure in the No. 1 oxygen tank continued to drift downward; passing 300 psi, now heading toward 200 psi. Months later, after the accident investigation was complete, it was determined that, when the No. 2 tank blew up, it either ruptured a line on the No. 1 tank, or caused one of the valves to leak. When the pressure reached 200 psi, the crew and ground controllers knew that they would lose all oxygen, which meant that the last fuel cell would also die.

9   At 1 hour and 29 seconds after the bang, Jack Lousma, then CapCom, said after instructions from Flight Director Glynn Lunney: "It is slowly going to zero, and we are starting to think about the LM lifeboat." Swigert replied, "That's what we have been thinking about too."

10   Ground controllers in Houston faced a **formidable** task. Completely new procedures had to be written and tested in the simulator before being passed up to the crew. The navigation problem had to be solved; essentially how, when, and in what altitude to burn the LM descent engine to provide a quick return home.

11   With only 15 minutes of power left in the CM, CapCom told the crew to make their way into the LM. Fred and Jim Lovell quickly floated through the tunnel, leaving Jack to perform the last chores in the Command Module. The first concern was to determine if there were enough consumables to get home? The LM was built for only a 45-hour lifetime, and it needed to be stretched to 90. Oxygen wasn't a problem. The full LM descent tank alone would **suffice**, and in addition, there were two ascent-engine oxygen tanks, and two backpacks whose oxygen supply would never be used on the lunar surface. Two emergency bottles on top of those packs had six or seven pounds each in them. (At LM jettison, just before reentry, 28.5 pounds of oxygen remained, more than half of what was available after the explosion).

12   Power was also a concern. There were 2181 ampere hours in the LM batteries, Ground controllers carefully worked out a procedure where the CM batteries were charged with LM power. All non-critical systems were turned off and

energy consumption was reduced to a fifth of normal, which resulted in having 20 percent of our LM electrical power left when Aquarius was jettisoned. There was one electrical close call during the mission. One of the CM batteries vented with such force that it momentarily dropped off the line. Had the battery failed, there would be insufficient power to return the ship to Earth.

13 Water was the main consumable concern. It was estimated that the crew would run out of water about five hours before Earth reentry, which was calculated at around 151 hours. However, data from *Apollo 11* (which had not sent its LM ascent stage crashing into the moon as in subsequent missions) showed that its mechanisms could survive seven or eight hours in space without water cooling. The crew conserved water. They cut down to six ounces each per day, a fifth of normal intake, and used fruit juices; they ate hot dogs and other wet-pack foods when they ate at all. The crew became dehydrated throughout the flight and set a record that stood up throughout *Apollo:* Lovell lost fourteen pounds, and the crew lost a total of 31.5 pounds, nearly 50 percent more than any other crew. Those stringent measures resulted in the crew finishing with 28.2 pounds of water, about 9 percent of the total.

14 Removal of Carbon Dioxide was also a concern. There were enough lithium hydroxide canisters, which remove carbon dioxide from the spacecraft, but the square canisters from the Command Module were not compatible with the round openings in the Lunar Module environmental system. There were four cartridge from the LM, and four from the backpacks, counting backups. However, the LM was designed to support two men for two days and was being asked to care for three men nearly four days. After a day and a half in the LM a warning light showed that the carbon dioxide had built up to a dangerous level. Mission Control **devised** a way to attach the CM canisters to the LM system by using plastic bags, cardboard, and tape- all materials carried on board.

15 One of the big questions was, "How to get back safely to Earth." The LM navigation system wasn't designed to help us in this situation. Before the explosion, at 30 hours and 40 minutes, Apollo 13 had made the normal midcourse correction, which would take it out of a free-return-to-Earth trajectory and put it on a lunar landing course. Now the task was to get back on a free-return course. The ground computed a 35-second burn and fired it 5 hours after the explosion. As they approached the moon, another burn was computed; this time a long 5-minute burn to speed up the return home. It took place 2 hours after rounding the far side of the moon.

• • •

16 The trip was marked by discomfort beyond the lack of food and water. Sleep was almost impossible because of the cold. When the electrical systems were turned off, the spacecraft lost an important source of heat. The temperature dropped to 38 F and condensation formed on all the walls.

17 A most remarkable achievement of Mission Control was quickly developing procedures for powering up the CM after its long cold sleep. Flight controllers wrote the documents for this innovation in three days, instead of the usual three months. The Command Module was cold and clammy at the start of power up. The walls, ceiling, floor, wire harnesses, and panels were all covered with droplets of water. It was suspected conditions were the same behind the panels. The chances of short circuits caused apprehension, but thanks to the safeguards built into the command module after the disastrous *Apollo 1* fire in January 1967, no arcing took place. The droplets furnished one sensation as we decelerated in the atmosphere: it rained inside the CM.

18 Four hours before landing, the crew shed the service module; Mission Control had insisted on retaining it until then because everyone feared what the cold of space might do to the unsheltered CM heat shield. Photos of the Service Module showed one whole panel missing, and wreckage hanging out, it was a sorry mess as it drifted away. Three hours later the crew left the Lunar Module Aquarius and then splashed down gently in the Pacific Ocean near Samoa.

 THINK QUESTIONS CA-CCSS: CA.RI.7.1, CA.L.7.4a, CA.L.7.4d

1. What words, phrases, or clues in the first two paragraphs help readers determine the subject (or content) area of the text? Cite specific textual evidence to support your answer.

2. What is the impact of technical language on the tone of the text? Cite specific evidence from the text to support your answer.

3. How effective is the use of technical language in the text? Cite specific textual evidence to support your answer.

4. Use context clues to determine the meaning of the word **formidable** as it is used in paragraph 10 of the text. Write your definition of "formidable" and identify the context clues you used to figure out the meaning of the word.

5. Use context clues to determine the meaning of **devised** in paragraph 14. Write your definition of "devised" and identify the context clues you used in the text to determine its meaning. Confirm your definition by looking up "devise" in the dictionary. Revise your definition as needed.

CLOSE READ

CA-CCSS: CA.RI.7.1, CA.RI.7.2, CA.RI.7.4; CA.L.7.4b, CA.L.7.6, CA.SL.7.1a, CA.W.7.2.a, CA.W.7.2.b, CA.W.7.2.c, CA.W.7.2.d, CA.W.7.2.e, CA.W.7.2.f, CA.W.7.4, CA.W.7.5, CA.W.7.6, CA.W.7.10

Reread the excerpt from *Apollo 13: Mission Highlights*. As you reread, complete the Focus Questions below. Then use your answers and annotations from the questions to help you complete the Writing Prompt.

 FOCUS QUESTIONS

1. As you reread the first three paragraphs, highlight the names of the two spacecraft in which the astronauts are working and living. Highlight, too, how the text helps readers understand the differences between the two spacecraft. What context clues in paragraph 3, including any Greek or Latin prefixes, suffixes, or roots of words, help readers understand the technical information and technical language in paragraph 2? Highlight specific textual evidence, and make annotations to explain your responses.

2. In paragraph 4, Lovell tells Houston that the problem is with a "main B bus undervolt." What clues in paragraph 3 help you infer what the "main B bus undervolt" supplies? Highlight textual evidence in paragraph 5, and make annotations citing the other technical problems that the spacecraft is experiencing.

3. Why was the removal of carbon dioxide from the LM a problem in paragraph 14? How did Mission Control solve the problem? Highlight specific technical language, including any Greek or Latin prefixes, suffixes, or roots of words, that helped you understand the technical information and technical language in the paragraph. Make annotations to help support your response.

4. In paragraph 17, the text states, "A most remarkable achievement of Mission Control was quickly developing procedures for powering up the CM after its long cold sleep." What did flight controllers do to solve the problem? Highlight specific technical language and evidence in the text, and make annotations explaining your response.

5. *Apollo's 13's* original mission was to explore a lunar highland, but after the explosion and failure of the spacecraft's oxygen tanks, the astronauts and mission control had a new goal in mind. What was this goal? Was it accomplished? Highlight specific evidence in paragraphs 15 and 18, and make annotations to explain your answers.

WRITING PROMPT

The *Apollo 13* mission has been called a "successful failure." Explain why in an informative/explanatory essay. Begin with a clear thesis statement. Organize your information and supporting details, citing specific textual evidence from "*Apollo 13:* Mission Highlights." Use technical language in your essay. Be sure to explain the meaning of scientific and technical terms, either by providing explicit evidence in the text or by using context clues to help readers draw inferences about the meaning of the terms. Clarify the connections among your ideas with transitions, and use a formal style suited to audience and purpose. Summarize your main ideas with a strong concluding statement.

RIKKI-TIKKI-TAVI

FICTION

Rudyard Kipling
1894

INTRODUCTION

"Rikki-Tikki-Tavi" is one of the most famous tales from *The Jungle Book*, a collection of short stories published in 1894 by English author Rudyard Kipling. The stories in *The Jungle Book* feature animal characters with anthropomorphic traits and are intended to be read as fables, each illustrating a moral lesson. In this story, Rikki-Tikki-Tavi is a courageous young mongoose adopted as a pet by a British family living in 19th-century colonial India.

"Rikki-tikki licked his lips.
'This is a splendid hunting-ground.'"

 FIRST READ

1   This is the story of the great war that Rikki-tikki-tavi fought single-handed, through the bath-rooms of the big bungalow in Segowlee cantonment. Darzee, the Tailorbird, helped him, and Chuchundra, the musk-rat, who never comes out into the middle of the floor, but always creeps round by the wall, gave him advice, but Rikki-tikki did the real fighting.

2   He was a mongoose, rather like a little cat in his fur and his tail, but quite like a weasel in his head and his habits. His eyes and the end of his **restless** nose were pink. He could scratch himself anywhere he pleased with any leg, front or back, that he chose to use. He could fluff up his tail till it looked like a bottle brush, and his war cry as he **scuttled** through the long grass was: "Rikk-tikk-tikki-tikki-tchk!"

3   One day, a high summer flood washed him out of the burrow where he lived with his father and mother, and carried him, kicking and clucking, down a roadside ditch. He found a little wisp of grass floating there, and clung to it till he lost his senses. When he revived, he was lying in the hot sun on the middle of a garden path, very draggled indeed, and a small boy was saying, "Here's a dead mongoose. Let's have a funeral."

4   "No," said his mother, "let's take him in and dry him. Perhaps he isn't really dead."

5   They took him into the house, and a big man picked him up between his finger and thumb and said he was not dead but half choked. So they wrapped him in cotton wool, and warmed him over a little fire, and he opened his eyes and sneezed.

6   "Now," said the big man (he was an Englishman who had just moved into the bungalow), "don't frighten him, and we'll see what he'll do."

Copyright © BookheadEd Learning, LLC

7   It is the hardest thing in the world to frighten a mongoose, because he is eaten up from nose to tail with curiosity. The motto of all the mongoose family is "Run and find out," and Rikki-tikki was a true mongoose. He looked at the cotton wool, decided that it was not good to eat, ran all round the table, sat up and put his fur in order, scratched himself, and jumped on the small boy's shoulder.

8   "Don't be frightened, Teddy," said his father. "That's his way of making friends."

9   "Ouch! He's tickling under my chin," said Teddy.

10   Rikki-tikki looked down between the boy's collar and neck, snuffed at his ear, and climbed down to the floor, where he sat rubbing his nose.

11   "Good gracious," said Teddy's mother, "and that's a wild creature! I suppose he's so tame because we've been kind to him."

12   "All mongooses are like that," said her husband. "If Teddy doesn't pick him up by the tail, or try to put him in a cage, he'll run in and out of the house all day long. Let's give him something to eat."

13   They gave him a little piece of raw meat. Rikki-tikki liked it immensely, and when it was finished he went out into the veranda and sat in the sunshine and fluffed up his fur to make it dry to the roots. Then he felt better.

14   "There are more things to find out about in this house," he said to himself, "than all my family could find out in all their lives. I shall certainly stay and find out."

15   He spent all that day roaming over the house. He nearly drowned himself in the bath-tubs, put his nose into the ink on a writing table, and burned it on the end of the big man's cigar, for he climbed up in the big man's lap to see how writing was done. At nightfall he ran into Teddy's nursery to watch how kerosene lamps were lighted, and when Teddy went to bed Rikki-tikki climbed up too. But he was a restless companion, because he had to get up and attend to every noise all through the night, and find out what made it. Teddy's mother and father came in, the last thing, to look at their boy, and Rikki-tikki was awake on the pillow. "I don't like that," said Teddy's mother. "He may bite the child." "He'll do no such thing," said the father. "Teddy's safer with that little beast than if he had a bloodhound to watch him. If a snake came into the nursery now—"

16   But Teddy's mother wouldn't think of anything so awful.

17   Early in the morning Rikki-tikki came to early breakfast in the veranda riding on Teddy's shoulder, and they gave him banana and some boiled egg. He sat

on all their laps one after the other, because every well-brought-up mongoose always hopes to be a house mongoose some day and have rooms to run about in; and Rikki-tikki's mother (she used to live in the general's house at Segowlee) had carefully told Rikki what to do if ever he came across white men.

18   Then Rikki-tikki went out into the garden to see what was to be seen. It was a large garden, only half cultivated, with bushes, as big as summer-houses, of Marshal Niel roses, lime and orange trees, clumps of bamboos, and thickets of high grass. Rikki-tikki licked his lips. "This is a splendid hunting-ground," he said, and his tail grew bottle-brushy at the thought of it, and he scuttled up and down the garden, snuffing here and there till he heard very sorrowful voices in a thorn-bush.

19   It was Darzee, the Tailorbird, and his wife. They had made a beautiful nest by pulling two big leaves together and stitching them up the edges with fibers, and had filled the hollow with cotton and downy fluff. The nest swayed to and fro, as they sat on the rim and cried.

20   "What is the matter?" asked Rikki-tikki.

21   "We are very miserable," said Darzee. "One of our babies fell out of the nest yesterday and Nag ate him."

22   "H'm!" said Rikki-tikki, "that is very sad—but I am a stranger here. Who is Nag?"

23   Darzee and his wife only cowered down in the nest without answering, for from the thick grass at the foot of the bush there came a low hiss—a horrid cold sound that made Rikki-tikki jump back two clear feet. Then inch by inch out of the grass rose up the head and spread hood of Nag, the big black cobra, and he was five feet long from tongue to tail. When he had lifted one-third of himself clear of the ground, he stayed balancing to and fro exactly as a dandelion tuft balances in the wind, and he looked at Rikki-tikki with the wicked snake's eyes that never change their expression, whatever the snake may be thinking of.

24   "Who is Nag?" said he. "I am Nag. The great God Brahm put his mark upon all our people, when the first cobra spread his hood to keep the sun off Brahm as he slept. Look, and be afraid!"

25   He spread out his hood more than ever, and Rikki-tikki saw the spectacle-mark on the back of it that looks exactly like the eye part of a hook-and-eye fastening. He was afraid for the minute, but it is impossible for a mongoose to stay frightened for any length of time, and though Rikki-tikki had never met a live cobra before, his mother had fed him on dead ones, and he knew that all a

grown mongoose's business in life was to fight and eat snakes. Nag knew that too and, at the bottom of his cold heart, he was afraid.

26   "Well," said Rikki-tikki, and his tail began to fluff up again, "marks or no marks, do you think it is right for you to eat fledglings out of a nest?"

27   Nag was thinking to himself, and watching the least little movement in the grass behind Rikki-tikki. He knew that mongooses in the garden meant death sooner or later for him and his family, but he wanted to get Rikki-tikki off his guard. So he dropped his head a little, and put it on one side.

28   "Let us talk," he said. "You eat eggs. Why should not I eat birds?"

29   "Behind you! Look behind you!" sang Darzee.

30   Rikki-tikki knew better than to waste time in staring. He jumped up in the air as high as he could go, and just under him whizzed by the head of Nagaina, Nag's wicked wife. She had crept up behind him as he was talking, to make an end of him. He heard her savage hiss as the stroke missed. He came down almost across her back, and if he had been an old mongoose he would have known that then was the time to break her back with one bite; but he was afraid of the terrible lashing return stroke of the cobra. He bit, indeed, but did not bite long enough, and he jumped clear of the whisking tail, leaving Nagaina torn and angry.

31   "Wicked, wicked Darzee!" said Nag, lashing up as high as he could reach toward the nest in the thorn-bush. But Darzee had built it out of reach of snakes, and it only swayed to and fro.

32   Rikki-tikki felt his eyes growing red and hot (when a mongoose's eyes grow red, he is angry), and he sat back on his tail and hind legs like a little kangaroo, and looked all round him, and chattered with rage. But Nag and Nagaina had disappeared into the grass. When a snake misses its stroke, it never says anything or gives any sign of what it means to do next. Rikki-tikki did not care to follow them, for he did not feel sure that he could manage two snakes at once. So he trotted off to the gravel path near the house, and sat down to think. It was a serious matter for him.

33   If you read the old books of natural history, you will find they say that when the mongoose fights the snake and happens to get bitten, he runs off and eats some herb that cures him. That is not true. The victory is only a matter of quickness of eye and quickness of foot—snake's blow against mongoose's jump—and as no eye can follow the motion of a snake's head when it strikes, this makes things much more wonderful than any magic herb. Rikki-tikki knew he was a young mongoose, and it made him all the more pleased to think that he had managed to escape a blow from behind. It gave him confidence in

himself, and when Teddy came running down the path, Rikki-tikki was ready to be petted.

34   But just as Teddy was stooping, something wriggled a little in the dust, and a tiny voice said: "Be careful. I am Death!" It was Karait, the dusty brown snakeling that lies for choice on the dusty earth; and his bite is as dangerous as the cobra's. But he is so small that nobody thinks of him, and so he does the more harm to people.

35   Rikki-tikki's eyes grew red again, and he danced up to Karait with the peculiar rocking, swaying motion that he had inherited from his family. It looks very funny, but it is so perfectly balanced a gait that you can fly off from it at any angle you please, and in dealing with snakes this is an advantage. If Rikki-tikki had only known, he was doing a much more dangerous thing than fighting Nag, for Karait is so small, and can turn so quickly, that unless Rikki bit him close to the back of the head, he would get the return stroke in his eye or his lip. But Rikki did not know. His eyes were all red, and he rocked back and forth, looking for a good place to hold. Karait struck out. Rikki jumped sideways and tried to run in, but the wicked little dusty gray head lashed within a fraction of his shoulder, and he had to jump over the body, and the head followed his heels close.

36   Teddy shouted to the house: "Oh, look here! Our mongoose is killing a snake." And Rikki-tikki heard a scream from Teddy's mother. His father ran out with a stick, but by the time he came up, Karait had lunged out once too far, and Rikki-tikki had sprung, jumped on the snake's back, dropped his head far between his forelegs, bitten as high up the back as he could get hold, and rolled away. That bite paralyzed Karait, and Rikki-tikki was just going to eat him up from the tail, after the custom of his family at dinner, when he remembered that a full meal makes a slow mongoose, and if he wanted all his strength and quickness ready, he must keep himself thin.

37   He went away for a dust bath under the castor-oil bushes, while Teddy's father beat the dead Karait. "What is the use of that?" thought Rikki-tikki. "I have settled it all;" and then Teddy's mother picked him up from the dust and hugged him, crying that he had saved Teddy from death, and Teddy's father said that he was a **providence,** and Teddy looked on with big scared eyes. Rikki-tikki was rather amused at all the fuss, which, of course, he did not understand. Teddy's mother might just as well have petted Teddy for playing in the dust. Rikki was thoroughly enjoying himself.

38   That night at dinner, walking to and fro among the wine-glasses on the table, he might have stuffed himself three times over with nice things. But he remembered Nag and Nagaina, and though it was very pleasant to be patted and petted by Teddy's mother, and to sit on Teddy's shoulder, his eyes would

get red from time to time, and he would go off into his long war cry of "Rikk-tikk-tikki-tikki-tchk!"

39   Teddy carried him off to bed, and insisted on Rikki-tikki sleeping under his chin. Rikki-tikki was too well bred to bite or scratch, but as soon as Teddy was asleep he went off for his nightly walk round the house, and in the dark he ran up against Chuchundra, the musk-rat, creeping around by the wall. Chuchundra is a broken-hearted little beast. He whimpers and cheeps all the night, trying to make up his mind to run into the middle of the room. But he never gets there.

40   "Don't kill me," said Chuchundra, almost weeping. "Rikki-tikki, don't kill me!"

41   "Do you think a snake-killer kills muskrats?" said Rikki-tikki scornfully.

42   "Those who kill snakes get killed by snakes," said Chuchundra, more sorrowfully than ever. "And how am I to be sure that Nag won't mistake me for you some dark night?"

43   "There's not the least danger," said Rikki-tikki. "But Nag is in the garden, and I know you don't go there."

44   "My cousin Chua, the rat, told me--" said Chuchundra, and then he stopped.

45   "Told you what?"

46   "H'sh! Nag is everywhere, Rikki-tikki. You should have talked to Chua in the garden."

47   "I didn't—so you must tell me. Quick, Chuchundra, or I'll bite you!"

48   Chuchundra sat down and cried till the tears rolled off his whiskers. "I am a very poor man," he sobbed. "I never had spirit enough to run out into the middle of the room. H'sh! I mustn't tell you anything. Can't you hear, Rikki-tikki?"

49   Rikki-tikki listened. The house was as still as still, but he thought he could just catch the faintest scratch-scratch in the world--a noise as faint as that of a wasp walking on a window-pane--the dry scratch of a snake's scales on brick-work.

50   "That's Nag or Nagaina," he said to himself, "and he is crawling into the bath-room sluice. You're right, Chuchundra; I should have talked to Chua."

51   He stole off to Teddy's bath-room, but there was nothing there, and then to Teddy's mother's bathroom. At the bottom of the smooth plaster wall there was a brick pulled out to make a sluice for the bath water, and as Rikki-tikki

stole in by the masonry curb where the bath is put, he heard Nag and Nagaina whispering together outside in the moonlight.

52 "When the house is emptied of people," said Nagaina to her husband, "he will have to go away, and then the garden will be our own again. Go in quietly, and remember that the big man who killed Karait is the first one to bite. Then come out and tell me, and we will hunt for Rikki-tikki together."

53 "But are you sure that there is anything to be gained by killing the people?" said Nag.

54 "Everything. When there were no people in the bungalow, did we have any mongoose in the garden? So long as the bungalow is empty, we are king and queen of the garden; and remember that as soon as our eggs in the melon bed hatch (as they may tomorrow), our children will need room and quiet."

55 "I had not thought of that," said Nag. "I will go, but there is no need that we should hunt for Rikki-tikki afterward. I will kill the big man and his wife, and the child if I can, and come away quietly. Then the bungalow will be empty, and Rikki-tikki will go."

56 Rikki-tikki tingled all over with rage and hatred at this, and then Nag's head came through the sluice, and his five feet of cold body followed it. Angry as he was, Rikki-tikki was very frightened as he saw the size of the big cobra. Nag coiled himself up, raised his head, and looked into the bathroom in the dark, and Rikki could see his eyes glitter.

57 "Now, if I kill him here, Nagaina will know; and if I fight him on the open floor, the odds are in his favor. What am I to do?" said Rikki-tikki-tavi.

58 Nag waved to and fro, and then Rikki-tikki heard him drinking from the biggest water-jar that was used to fill the bath. "That is good," said the snake. "Now, when Karait was killed, the big man had a stick. He may have that stick still, but when he comes in to bathe in the morning he will not have a stick. I shall wait here till he comes. Nagaina—do you hear me?—I shall wait here in the cool till daytime."

59 There was no answer from outside, so Rikki-tikki knew Nagaina had gone away. Nag coiled himself down, coil by coil, round the bulge at the bottom of the water jar, and Rikki-tikki stayed still as death. After an hour he began to move, muscle by muscle, toward the jar. Nag was asleep, and Rikki-tikki looked at his big back, wondering which would be the best place for a good hold. "If I don't break his back at the first jump," said Rikki, "he can still fight. And if he fights—O Rikki!" He looked at the thickness of the neck below the hood, but that was too much for him; and a bite near the tail would only make Nag savage.

60   "It must be the head"' he said at last; "the head above the hood. And, when I am once there, I must not let go."

61   Then he jumped. The head was lying a little clear of the water jar, under the curve of it; and, as his teeth met, Rikki braced his back against the bulge of the red earthenware to hold down the head. This gave him just one second's purchase, and he made the most of it. Then he was battered to and fro as a rat is shaken by a dog—to and fro on the floor, up and down, and around in great circles, but his eyes were red and he held on as the body cart-whipped over the floor, upsetting the tin dipper and the soap dish and the flesh brush, and banged against the tin side of the bath. As he held he closed his jaws tighter and tighter, for he made sure he would be banged to death, and, for the honor of his family, he preferred to be found with his teeth locked. He was dizzy, aching, and felt shaken to pieces when something went off like a thunderclap just behind him. A hot wind knocked him senseless and red fire singed his fur. The big man had been wakened by the noise, and had fired both barrels of a shotgun into Nag just behind the hood.

62   Rikki-tikki held on with his eyes shut, for now he was quite sure he was dead. But the head did not move, and the big man picked him up and said, "It's the mongoose again, Alice. The little chap has saved our lives now."

63   Then Teddy's mother came in with a very white face, and saw what was left of Nag, and Rikki-tikki dragged himself to Teddy's bedroom and spent half the rest of the night shaking himself tenderly to find out whether he really was broken into forty pieces, as he fancied.

64   When morning came he was very stiff, but well pleased with his doings. "Now I have Nagaina to settle with, and she will be worse than five Nags, and there's no knowing when the eggs she spoke of will hatch. Goodness! I must go and see Darzee," he said.

65   Without waiting for breakfast, Rikki-tikki ran to the thornbush where Darzee was singing a song of triumph at the top of his voice. The news of Nag's death was all over the garden, for the sweeper had thrown the body on the rubbish-heap.

66   "Oh, you stupid tuft of feathers!" said Rikki-tikki angrily. "Is this the time to sing?"

67   "Nag is dead—is dead—is dead!" sang Darzee. "The **valiant** Rikki-tikki caught him by the head and held fast. The big man brought the bang-stick, and Nag fell in two pieces! He will never eat my babies again."

68   "All that's true enough. But where's Nagaina?" said Rikki-tikki, looking carefully round him.

69   "Nagaina came to the bathroom sluice and called for Nag," Darzee went on, "and Nag came out on the end of a stick—the sweeper picked him up on the end of a stick and threw him upon the rubbish heap. Let us sing about the great, the red-eyed Rikki-tikki!" And Darzee filled his throat and sang.

70   "If I could get up to your nest, I'd roll your babies out!" said Rikki-tikki. "You don't know when to do the right thing at the right time. You're safe enough in your nest there, but it's war for me down here. Stop singing a minute, Darzee."

71   "For the great, the beautiful Rikki-tikki's sake I will stop," said Darzee. "What is it, O Killer of the terrible Nag?"

72   "Where is Nagaina, for the third time?"

73   "On the rubbish heap by the stables, mourning for Nag. Great is Rikki-tikki with the white teeth."

74   "Bother my white teeth! Have you ever heard where she keeps her eggs?"

75   "In the melon bed, on the end nearest the wall, where the sun strikes nearly all day. She hid them there weeks ago."

76   "And you never thought it worth while to tell me? The end nearest the wall, you said?"

77   "Rikki-tikki, you are not going to eat her eggs?"

78   "Not eat exactly; no. Darzee, if you have a grain of sense you will fly off to the stables and pretend that your wing is broken, and let Nagaina chase you away to this bush. I must get to the melon-bed, and if I went there now she'd see me."

79   Darzee was a feather-brained little fellow who could never hold more than one idea at a time in his head. And just because he knew that Nagaina's children were born in eggs like his own, he didn't think at first that it was fair to kill them. But his wife was a sensible bird, and she knew that cobra's eggs meant young cobras later on. So she flew off from the nest, and left Darzee to keep the babies warm, and continue his song about the death of Nag. Darzee was very like a man in some ways.

80   She fluttered in front of Nagaina by the rubbish heap and cried out, "Oh, my wing is broken! The boy in the house threw a stone at me and broke it." Then she fluttered more desperately than ever.

81 Nagaina lifted up her head and hissed, "You warned Rikki-tikki when I would have killed him. Indeed and truly, you've chosen a bad place to be lame in." And she moved toward Darzee's wife, slipping along over the dust.

82 "The boy broke it with a stone!" shrieked Darzee's wife.

83 "Well! It may be some **consolation** to you when you're dead to know that I shall settle accounts with the boy. My husband lies on the rubbish heap this morning, but before night the boy in the house will lie very still. What is the use of running away? I am sure to catch you. Little fool, look at me!"

84 Darzee's wife knew better than to do that, for a bird who looks at a snake's eyes gets so frightened that she cannot move. Darzee's wife fluttered on, piping sorrowfully, and never leaving the ground, and Nagaina quickened her pace.

85 Rikki-tikki heard them going up the path from the stables, and he raced for the end of the melon patch near the wall. There, in the warm litter above the melons, very cunningly hidden, he found twenty-five eggs, about the size of a bantam's eggs, but with whitish skin instead of shell.

86 "I was not a day too soon," he said, for he could see the baby cobras curled up inside the skin, and he knew that the minute they were hatched they could each kill a man or a mongoose. He bit off the tops of the eggs as fast as he could, taking care to crush the young cobras, and turned over the litter from time to time to see whether he had missed any. At last there were only three eggs left, and Rikki-tikki began to chuckle to himself, when he heard Darzee's wife screaming:

87 "Rikki-tikki, I led Nagaina toward the house, and she has gone into the veranda, and—oh, come quickly—she means killing!"

88 Rikki-tikki smashed two eggs, and tumbled backward down the melon-bed with the third egg in his mouth, and scuttled to the veranda as hard as he could put foot to the ground. Teddy and his mother and father were there at early breakfast, but Rikki-tikki saw that they were not eating anything. They sat stone-still, and their faces were white. Nagaina was coiled up on the matting by Teddy's chair, within easy striking distance of Teddy's bare leg, and she was swaying to and fro, singing a song of triumph.

89 "Son of the big man that killed Nag," she hissed, "stay still. I am not ready yet. Wait a little. Keep very still, all you three! If you move I strike, and if you do not move I strike. Oh, foolish people, who killed my Nag!"

90 Teddy's eyes were fixed on his father, and all his father could do was to whisper, "Sit still, Teddy. You mustn't move. Teddy, keep still."

91   Then Rikki-tikki came up and cried, "Turn round, Nagaina. Turn and fight!"

92   "All in good time," said she, without moving her eyes. "I will settle my account with you presently. Look at your friends, Rikki-tikki. They are still and white. They are afraid. They dare not move, and if you come a step nearer I strike."

93   "Look at your eggs," said Rikki-tikki, "in the melon bed near the wall. Go and look, Nagaina!"

94   The big snake turned half around, and saw the egg on the veranda. "Ah-h! Give it to me," she said.

95   Rikki-tikki put his paws one on each side of the egg, and his eyes were blood-red. "What price for a snake's egg? For a young cobra? For a young king cobra? For the last—the very last of the brood? The ants are eating all the others down by the melon bed."

96   Nagaina spun clear round, forgetting everything for the sake of the one egg. Rikki-tikki saw Teddy's father shoot out a big hand, catch Teddy by the shoulder, and drag him across the little table with the tea-cups, safe and out of reach of Nagaina.

97   "Tricked! Tricked! Tricked! Rikk-tck-tck!" chuckled Rikki-tikki. "The boy is safe, and it was I—I—I that caught Nag by the hood last night in the bathroom." Then he began to jump up and down, all four feet together, his head close to the floor. "He threw me to and fro, but he could not shake me off. He was dead before the big man blew him in two. I did it! Rikki-tikki-tck-tck! Come then, Nagaina. Come and fight with me. You shall not be a widow long."

98   Nagaina saw that she had lost her chance of killing Teddy, and the egg lay between Rikki-tikki's paws. "Give me the egg, Rikki-tikki. Give me the last of my eggs, and I will go away and never come back," she said, lowering her hood.

99   "Yes, you will go away, and you will never come back. For you will go to the rubbish heap with Nag. Fight, widow! The big man has gone for his gun! Fight!"

100   Rikki-tikki was bounding all round Nagaina, keeping just out of reach of her stroke, his little eyes like hot coals. Nagaina gathered herself together and flung out at him. Rikki-tikki jumped up and backward. Again and again and again she struck, and each time her head came with a whack on the matting of the veranda and she gathered herself together like a watch spring. Then Rikki-tikki danced in a circle to get behind her, and Nagaina spun round to keep her head to his head, so that the rustle of her tail on the matting sounded like dry leaves blown along by the wind.

Please note that excerpts and passages in the StudySync® library and this workbook are intended as touchstones to generate interest in an author's work. The excerpts and passages do not substitute for the reading of entire texts, and StudySync® strongly recommends that students seek out and purchase the whole literary or informational work in order to experience it as the author intended. Links to online resellers are available in our digital library. In addition, complete works may be ordered through an authorized reseller by filling out and returning to StudySync® the order form enclosed in this workbook.

NOTES

101 He had forgotten the egg. It still lay on the veranda, and Nagaina came nearer and nearer to it, till at last, while Rikki-tikki was drawing breath, she caught it in her mouth, turned to the veranda steps, and flew like an arrow down the path, with Rikki-tikki behind her. When the cobra runs for her life, she goes like a whip-lash flicked across a horse's neck.

102 Rikki-tikki knew that he must catch her, or all the trouble would begin again. She headed straight for the long grass by the thorn-bush, and as he was running Rikki-tikki heard Darzee still singing his foolish little song of triumph. But Darzee's wife was wiser. She flew off her nest as Nagaina came along, and flapped her wings about Nagaina's head. If Darzee had helped they might have turned her, but Nagaina only lowered her hood and went on. Still, the instant's delay brought Rikki-tikki up to her, and as she plunged into the rat-hole where she and Nag used to live, his little white teeth were clenched on her tail, and he went down with her—and very few mongooses, however wise and old they may be, care to follow a cobra into its hole. It was dark in the hole; and Rikki-tikki never knew when it might open out and give Nagaina room to turn and strike at him. He held on savagely, and stuck out his feet to act as brakes on the dark slope of the hot, moist earth.

103 Then the grass by the mouth of the hole stopped waving, and Darzee said, "It is all over with Rikki-tikki! We must sing his death song. Valiant Rikki-tikki is dead! For Nagaina will surely kill him underground."

104 So he sang a very mournful song that he made up on the spur of the minute, and just as he got to the most touching part, the grass quivered again, and Rikki-tikki, covered with dirt, dragged himself out of the hole leg by leg, licking his whiskers. Darzee stopped with a little shout. Rikki-tikki shook some of the dust out of his fur and sneezed. "It is all over," he said. "The widow will never come out again." And the red ants that live between the grass stems heard him, and began to troop down one after another to see if he had spoken the truth. Rikki-tikki curled himself up in the grass and slept where he was--slept and slept till it was late in the afternoon, for he had done a hard day's work.

105 "Now," he said, when he awoke, "I will go back to the house. Tell the Coppersmith, Darzee, and he will tell the garden that Nagaina is dead."

106 The Coppersmith is a bird who makes a noise exactly like the beating of a little hammer on a copper pot; and the reason he is always making it is because he is the town crier to every Indian garden, and tells all the news to everybody who cares to listen. As Rikki-tikki went up the path, he heard his "attention" notes like a tiny dinner gong, and then the steady "Ding-dong-tock! Nag is dead—dong! Nagaina is dead! Ding-dong-tock!" That set all the birds in the garden singing, and the frogs croaking, for Nag and Nagaina used to eat frogs as well as little birds.

NOTES

107   When Rikki got to the house, Teddy and Teddy's mother (she looked very white still, for she had been fainting) and Teddy's father came out and almost cried over him; and that night he ate all that was given him till he could eat no more, and went to bed on Teddy's shoulder, where Teddy's mother saw him when she came to look late at night.

108   "He saved our lives and Teddy's life," she said to her husband. "Just think, he saved all our lives."

109   Rikki-tikki woke up with a jump, for the mongooses are light sleepers.

110   "Oh, it's you," said he. "What are you bothering for? All the cobras are dead. And if they weren't, I'm here."

111   Rikki-tikki had a right to be proud of himself. But he did not grow too proud, and he kept that garden as a mongoose should keep it, with tooth and jump and spring and bite, till never a cobra dared show its head inside the walls.

THINK QUESTIONS   CA-CCSS: CA.RL.7.1, CA.L.7.4a, CA.L.7.4b, CA.SL.7.1a, CA.SL.7.1c, CA.SL.7.1d

1.   How did Rikki-tikki-tavi come to live with the English family? Cite specific evidence from the text to support your answer.

2.   How effectively does the description of Nag in paragraph 23 evoke the image that he is a snake to be feared? Cite specific evidence from the text to support your answer.

3.   What can you infer about Rikki-tikki's character by the fact that he has saved the family three times from snakes? How might his character and actions help readers infer the theme? Cite specific evidence from the text to support your inference.

4.   Use context to determine the meaning of the word **valiant** as it is used in paragraph 67 of "Rikki-Tikki-Tavi." Write your definition of "valiant" and tell how you determined the meaning of the word.

5.   By remembering that the Latin prefix *con-* means "with," the root *sol* means "comfort," and the suffix *-ation* means "the act of," how do the Latin prefix, root, and suffix provide clues to the meaning of **consolation?** Write your definition of "consolation" and tell how you figured out its meaning.

CLOSE READ

CA-CCSS: CA.RL.7.1, CA.RL.7.2, CA.RL.7.3, CA.L.7.4c, CA.W.7.2a, CA.W.7.2b, CA.W.7.4, CA.W.7.5, CA.W.7.6, CA.W.7.10

Reread the story "Rikki-Tikki-Tavi." As you reread, complete the Focus Questions below. Then use your answers and annotations from the questions to help you complete the Writing Prompt.

FOCUS QUESTIONS

1. As you reread "Rikki-Tikki-Tavi," highlight the words "frighten" and "frightened" as they are used in paragraphs 6–8 in the text. How does the repetition of the word indicate that fear or overcoming fear may be a clue to the main theme of the story? Make annotations outlining your ideas.

2. How does Rikki-tikki behave like a young child in paragraph 17? What might his behavior suggest about how he might change by the end of the story? Highlight words and phrases in the text that support your response. Make annotations to record your ideas.

3. Why does Darzee sing a death song when Rikki-tikki goes into Nagaina's burrow to try to kill her? What effect does the song have on the reader's expectation of what might happen to Rikki-tikki? Highlight evidence in the text to support your ideas, and make annotations to summarize your response.

4. Why is Rikki-tikki proud of himself in the last paragraph of the story? How does the last paragraph express how much he has grown up? Highlight the reasons for his proud feelings, as expressed by Teddy's mother. Make annotations listing some adjectives in a two-column chart to describe how Rikki-tikki was at the beginning of the story and how he has grown at the end. Use a print or digital dictionary to determine or clarify the precise meaning of each word and its part of speech as an adjective before you list it in the chart.

5. Why is Rikki-tikki so determined to undertake the mission of destroying Nag and Nagaina? What "big idea" or theme do his actions suggest? Highlight specific evidence from the text to support your statement of the theme. Then make annotations stating the theme in a few brief words.

WRITING PROMPT

A coming-of-age story focuses on the central idea or theme of a young person growing and changing by solving a problem, undertaking a mission, or accomplishing a goal. How could "Rikki-Tikki-Tavi" be considered a coming-of-age story? What problem does he solve, mission does he undertake, or goal does he accomplish by the end of the story? Cite specific evidence from the text to convey how his thoughts and actions change over the course of the text to demonstrate that he has grown up at the end.

Please note that excerpts and passages in the StudySync® library and this workbook are intended as touchstones to generate interest in an author's work. The excerpts and passages do not substitute for the reading of entire texts, and StudySync® strongly recommends that students seek out and purchase the whole literary or informational work in order to experience it as the author intended. Links to online resellers are available in our digital library. In addition, complete works may be ordered through an authorized reseller by filling out and returning to StudySync® the order form enclosed in this workbook.

Reading & Writing Companion

75

THE CALL OF THE WILD

FICTION

Jack London
1903

INTRODUCTION

Author Jack London (1876–1916) was a turn-of-the-century writer and adventurer, beginning his life on the San Francisco Bay, then travelling the world—seal hunting in the Far East, mucking for gold in the Yukon Territory, sailing the South Pacific, and more. While participating in the Klondike Gold Rush, he reportedly encountered a mythical wolf that served as the inspiration for *The Call of the Wild*, his most popular novel. The book details the adventures of Buck, a large and powerful St. Bernard mix, as he experiences both love and abuse from a succession of owners. In this excerpt, Buck, by now a sled-dog, stirs up rebellion among the team when he stands up to the aggressive alpha dog, Spitz.

"There is an ecstasy that marks the summit of life, and beyond which life cannot rise."

 FIRST READ

From Chapter III, The Dominant Primordial Beast

1   They made Sixty Mile, which is a fifty-mile run, on the first day; and the second day saw them booming up the Yukon well on their way to Pelly. But such splendid running was achieved not without great trouble and vexation on the part of Francois. The insidious revolt led by Buck had destroyed the **solidarity** of the team. It no longer was as one dog leaping in the traces. The encouragement Buck gave the rebels led them into all kinds of petty **misdemeanors**. No more was Spitz a leader greatly to be feared. The old awe departed, and they grew equal to challenging his authority. Pike robbed him of half a fish one night, and gulped it down under the protection of Buck. Another night Dub and Joe fought Spitz and made him forego the punishment they deserved. And even Billee, the good-natured, was less good-natured, and whined not half so **placatingly** as in former days. Buck never came near Spitz without snarling and bristling menacingly. In fact, his conduct approached that of a bully, and he was given to swaggering up and down before Spitz's very nose.

2   The breaking down of discipline likewise affected the dogs in their relations with one another. They quarrelled and bickered more than ever among themselves, till at times the camp was a howling bedlam. Dave and Sol-leks alone were unaltered, though they were made irritable by the unending squabbling. Francois swore strange barbarous oaths, and stamped the snow in futile rage, and tore his hair. His lash was always singing among the dogs, but it was of small avail. Directly his back was turned they were at it again. He backed up Spitz with his whip, while Buck backed up the remainder of the team. Francois knew he was behind all the trouble, and Buck knew he knew; but Buck was too clever ever again to be caught red-handed. He worked faithfully in the harness, for the toil had become a delight to him; yet it was a greater delight slyly to **precipitate** a fight amongst his mates and tangle the traces.

Please note that excerpts and passages in the StudySync® library and this workbook are intended as touchstones to generate interest in an author's work. The excerpts and passages do not substitute for the reading of entire texts, and StudySync® strongly recommends that students seek out and purchase the whole literary or informational work in order to experience it as the author intended. Links to online resellers are available in our digital library. In addition, complete works may be ordered through an authorized reseller by filling out and returning to StudySync® the order form enclosed in this workbook.

Reading & Writing Companion   77

3   At the mouth of the Tahkeena, one night after supper, Dub turned up a snowshoe rabbit, blundered it, and missed. In a second the whole team was in full cry. A hundred yards away was a camp of the Northwest Police, with fifty dogs, huskies all, who joined the chase. The rabbit sped down the river, turned off into a small creek, up the frozen bed of which it held steadily. It ran lightly on the surface of the snow, while the dogs ploughed through by main strength. Buck led the pack, sixty strong, around bend after bend, but he could not gain. He lay down low to the race, whining eagerly, his splendid body flashing forward, leap by leap, in the wan white moonlight. And leap by leap, like some pale frost wraith, the snowshoe rabbit flashed on ahead.

4   All that stirring of old instincts which at stated periods drives men out from the sounding cities to forest and plain to kill things by chemically propelled leaden pellets, the blood lust, the joy to kill--all this was Buck's, only it was infinitely more intimate. He was ranging at the head of the pack, running the wild thing down, the living meat, to kill with his own teeth and wash his muzzle to the eyes in warm blood.

5   There is an **ecstasy** that marks the summit of life, and beyond which life cannot rise. And such is the paradox of living, this ecstasy comes when one is most alive, and it comes as a complete forgetfulness that one is alive. This ecstasy, this forgetfulness of living, comes to the artist, caught up and out of himself in a sheet of flame; it comes to the soldier, war-mad on a stricken field and refusing quarter; and it came to Buck, leading the pack, sounding the old wolf-cry, straining after the food that was alive and that fled swiftly before him through the moonlight. He was sounding the deeps of his nature, and of the parts of his nature that were deeper than he, going back into the womb of Time. He was mastered by the sheer surging of life, the tidal wave of being, the perfect joy of each separate muscle, joint, and sinew in that it was everything that was not death, that it was aglow and rampant, expressing itself in movement, flying exultantly under the stars and over the face of dead matter that did not move.

THINK QUESTIONS CA-CCSS: CA.RL.7.1, CA.RL.7.4, CA.L.7.4a, CA.L.7.4b, CA.L.7.4d, CA.SL.7.1a, CA.SL.7.1c, CA.SL.7.1d, CA.SL.7.3, CA.SL.7.4

1. Refer to several details in the first paragraph to explain how Buck "destroyed the solidarity of the team." Cite evidence that is directly stated in the text, and also make inferences to support your explanation.

2. What evidence is there in paragraph 2 that Buck took pleasure in causing trouble for Francois? Cite specific evidence from the text.

3. How did Buck react when Dub turned up a snowshoe rabbit? What inferences can you make about Buck from his behavior? Support your answer with specific evidence from the text.

4. Use context to determine the meaning of the word **misdemeanors** as it is used in the first paragraph of *The Call of the Wild*. Write your definition of "misdemeanors" and tell how you determined the meaning of the word. Then check your definition in a print or digital dictionary to confirm the word's meaning.

5. By understanding that the Latin word *placare* means "to calm down" or "appease," use the context clues provided in the first paragraph to determine the meaning of **placatingly.** Write your definition of "placatingly" and tell how you determined the meaning of the word.

CLOSE READ
CA-CCSS: CA.RL.7.1, CA.RL.7.2, CA.RL.7.7, CA.W.7.2a, CA.W.7.2b, CA.W.7.2c, CA.W.7.2d, CA.W.7.2e, CA.W.7.2f, CA.W.7.4, CA.W.7.5, CA.W.7.6, CA.W.7.10

Reread the excerpt from *The Call of the Wild*. As you reread, complete the Focus Questions below. Then use your answers and annotations from the questions to help you complete the Writing Prompt.

FOCUS QUESTIONS

1. Listen to the audio recording of the first part of paragraph 2 (1:08–1:41). How does the actor (or speaker) use expression and intonation when he describes Francois' reaction to the the dogs' "unending squabbling"? Highlight textual evidence in paragraph 2 and annotate ideas from the audio recording to show the development of your understanding of media techniques.

2. Listen to the second part of the audio recording of paragraph 2 (1:42–2:00). How does the actor use expression and intonation to help listeners understand Francois' relationship with Buck? Highlight textual evidence in paragraph 2 and annotate ideas from the audio recording to show the development of your understanding of media techniques.

3. Listen to the audio recording of the second half of paragraph 3 (2:29–2:52). How does the actor use expression and pacing to convey Buck's pursuit of the snowshoe rabbit? Highlight textual evidence in paragraph 3 and annotate ideas from the audio recording to show the development of your understanding of media techniques.

4. Reread the last paragraph of the excerpt and then listen to the audio recording of the same paragraph. Use details from the audio version and the printed text to explain what the actor in the audio adds to the reader's understanding of the paragraph.

5. How does Buck's story help readers understand what drives individuals to undertake a mission? Highlight textual evidence and make annotations to support your response.

WRITING PROMPT

Compare and contrast the text and the audio versions of *The Call of the Wild*. Begin with a clear thesis statement that sets the direction for the rest of your writing. How are the two media alike, and how are they different? At what points does the audio version use expression, intonation, and /or pace to support or interpret the text? In what ways do these interpretations help to develop character, setting, plot, and theme? Using precise language and selection vocabulary, support your writing with evidence from the text and the audio file. Use transitions to show the relationships among your ideas. Present your information with a formal style. Summarize your main points in a conclusion that supports the ideas you have presented.

READY FOR MARCOS

English Language Development

FICTION

INTRODUCTION

Twelve-year-old Monica Alvarez has a happy life. She is a star on the track team and has many good friends. But everything changes when her parents bring Marcos, her new baby brother, home from the hospital. Her parents want her to have more responsibilities. Monica wonders what it will mean to be a big sister. Is she ready? Is she willing?

"Monica wondered how someone so small could justify such trouble."

 FIRST READ

1 Three days ago her parents brought her new brother home from the hospital. Monica had known about him, but she hadn't thought about how her life would change. Yet, from the moment her mom and dad walked through the door cradling their football-sized bundle, everything was different. Her parents drifted **aimlessly** through the day as if in a fog. They used to be energetic and **vivacious,** but now they always seemed fatigued.

2 On Marcos's fourth day home, Monica woke up to the sound of her parents talking quietly. She **covertly** tiptoed to the door. "Monica is a big sister now," her dad said. "I think it's time for her to have more responsibilities at home."

3 Her mom agreed. "We'll talk at dinner," she added.

4 Monica turned and walked back to her room. *More responsibilities?* she thought to herself. *I already have a lot to do!*

5 She passed the afternoon thinking how the new baby would change her life. This year she was one of the fastest seventh graders on the track team. With more responsibilities, could she still **pursue** her dream of making the eighth-grade team? And what about time for her friends? What would she have to give up?

6 Later, as dinner time was nearing, Monica began to dread the talk with her parents. She could hear them in the kitchen, so she went into Marcos's room, where he lay sleeping in his crib. Her new little brother—Marcos.

7 Monica wondered how someone so small could **justify** such trouble. For the first time, she looked closely at him. He was so small, but she could see that he had the Alvarez nose. She ran her finger down Marcos's soft cheek. *He's really little and cute*, Monica thought. Suddenly, Marcos opened his tiny eyes

and gazed up at her. As she looked at him, Monica felt a **subtle** change. She had felt in **turmoil** before, but now she felt something new. She was a big sister. She knew how to tie her shoes and ride a bike, but Marcos would need someone to show him everything.

8   As Monica sat down to dinner, she felt her courage rising. "Mom, Dad, I have something to say," she began. "I'm a big sister now, and I should help more." Her parents glanced at each other. "I've done laundry lots of times," Monica explained, "and now I can do it for you and Marcos, too. I could get up a little earlier on weekends to make a little extra time. Plus, I can help with dinner after track practice. And when Marcos is bigger, I can teach him things."

9   Her mom smiled and exclaimed, "You're going to be the best big sister!"

 USING LANGUAGE   CA-CCSS: ELD.PII.7.2.a.Ex

Read each sentence. For numbers 1–2, look at the underlined pronoun. Use the clues in the sentence to determine what the pronoun refers to. For numbers 3–5, select a synonym for the underlined adjective. Be careful not to change the meaning of each sentence.

1. Later, as dinner time approached, Monica began to dread the upcoming discussion with her parents. <u>She</u> could hear them in the kitchen.

    ○ parents   ○ Monica

2. She ducked into Marcos's room where <u>he</u> was sleeping in his crib. Her little brother. Marcos.

    ○ Marcos   ○ Monica

3. Monica wondered how someone so <u>small</u> could justify such trouble.

    ○ tiny   ○ sleepy

4. As she looked at him, Monica felt a <u>subtle</u> change.

    ○ very noticeable   ○ very slight

5. As Monica sat down to dinner, she felt <u>rising</u> courage.

    ○ growing   ○ failing

Please note that excerpts and passages in the StudySync® library and this workbook are intended as touchstones to generate interest in an author's work. The excerpts and passages do not substitute for the reading of entire texts, and StudySync® strongly recommends that students seek out and purchase the whole literary or informational work in order to experience it as the author intended. Links to online resellers are available in our digital library. In addition, complete works may be ordered through an authorized reseller by filling out and returning to StudySync® the order form enclosed in this workbook.

Reading & Writing Companion   83

MEANINGFUL INTERACTIONS   CA-CCSS: ELD.PII.7.1.Ex

Work with your partner to fill in the sequence words to show how the events unfold in the story. You may refer back to each paragraph in the text to find these sequence words. Then complete the last sentence to explain how the story is ordered. Use the self-assessment rubric to evaluate your participation in the activity.

1 _____ her parents brought her new brother home from the hospital.

6 _____, Monica began to dread the talk with her parents.

7 She wondered how someone so small could justify such trouble.

_____, she looked closely at him.

_____, Monica felt a subtle change.

8 _____, she felt her courage rising.

I know this story is written in _____ order because events happen _____.

SELF-ASSESSMENT RUBRIC   CA-CCSS: ELD.PII.7.1.Ex

	4 I did this well.	3 I did this pretty well.	2 I did this a little bit.	1 I did not do this.
I took an active part with a partner in doing the assigned task.				
I contributed effectively to the decisions.				
I understood the use of sequence words in the selection.				
I helped a partner understand the use of sequence words in the selection.				
I completed the sentences carefully and accurately to show the text sequence.				

REREAD

Reread "Ready for Marcos." After you reread, complete the Using Language and Meaningful Interactions activities.

 ## USING LANGUAGE CA-CCSS: ELD.PII.7.1.Ex

Look at the story structure shown in the chart. Write the events of the story in the correct box to show the sequence of events.

Key Event Options
"Monica is a big sister now," her dad said, "I think it's time for her to have more responsibilities at home." Her mom agreed.
Marcos opened his tiny eyes and gazed up at her.
Three days ago her parents brought her new brother home from the hospital.
"Mom, Dad, I have something to say," she began. "I'm a big sister now, and I should help more."
As she looked at him, Monica felt a subtle change.

Story Structure	Key Event
Exposition	
Chronological Event	
Chronological Event	
Chronological Event	
Resolution	

👥 MEANINGFUL INTERACTIONS CA-CCSS: ELD.PI.7.6.b.Ex

In "Ready for Marcos," we see firsthand the inner struggle Monica goes through upon the arrival of her new baby brother, Marcos. Work with a partner or in a small group to observe some of Monica's thoughts and behaviors and make inferences about the text. Then use the self-assessment rubric to evaluate your participation in the discussion.

- One thing I observe about Monica is . . .

- I think this can mean . . .

- From this observation, I infer . . .   because . . .

- Another thing I observe about Monica is . . .

- I think this can mean . . .

- From this observation, I infer . . .   because . . .

SELF-ASSESSMENT RUBRIC CA-CCSS: ELD.PI.7.6.b.Ex

	4 I did this well.	3 I did this pretty well.	2 I did this a little bit.	1 I did not do this.
I expressed my inferences clearly.				
I listened carefully to others' inferences.				
I spoke respectfully when disagreeing with others.				
I was courteous when sharing my inferences with others.				

REREAD

Reread paragraphs 1–2 of "Ready for Marcos." After you reread, complete the Using Language and Meaningful Interactions activities.

 USING LANGUAGE CA-CCSS: ELD.PI.7.12.b.Ex

Select the affix that changes the word indicated in each sentence.

1. Select the affix that changes the verb to past tense: Noely <u>walked</u> to school yesterday.

    ○ -ed
    ○ wa-

2. Select the affix that makes the word an adverb: Emmanuel ran the race <u>quickly</u>.

    ○ qu-
    ○ -ly

3. Select the affix that makes the word mean the opposite: Don't treat others in an <u>unkind</u> way.

    ○ un-
    ○ -nd

4. Select the affix that shows Jennifer is listening right now: Jennifer is <u>listening</u> to music.

    ○ list-
    ○ -ing

5. Select the affix that means "again": They had to <u>restart</u> the engine.

    ○ re-
    ○ -art

Please note that excerpts and passages in the StudySync® library and this workbook are intended as touchstones to generate interest in an author's work. The excerpts and passages do not substitute for the reading of entire texts, and StudySync® strongly recommends that students seek out and purchase the whole literary or informational work in order to experience it as the author intended. Links to online resellers are available in our digital library. In addition, complete works may be ordered through an authorized reseller by filling out and returning to StudySync® the order form enclosed in this workbook.

Reading & Writing
Companion

87

MEANINGFUL INTERACTIONS CA-CCSS: ELD.PI.7.11.b.Ex

At the beginning of "Ready for Marcos," Monica is not sure how she feels about having more responsibilities around the house. She knows her parents want her to help, but she worries she will not have time for her own interests. Work with a partner or in a small group to discuss reasons for and against Monica's having more responsibilities. Then, write an opinion statement about whether it is right for Monica to have more responsibilities. Temper your opinions with modal expressions such as "could/would/should," "likely," and "possibly." Use the writing frames below. Be prepared to present your opinion statement to the class.

- In my opinion, Monica should / should not _____
_____.

- This is my opinion because she may _____
_____.

- It's possible that _____
_____.

- Another reason for my opinion is _____
_____.

- She _____
_____.

- In conclusion, I think Monica should / should not have more responsibilities because _____
_____.

A WORLD AWAY

English Language
Development

FICTION

INTRODUCTION

As Rajeet Basak was about to begin seventh grade in Mumbai, India, his family moved to Chicago, Illinois, for his father's work. Rajeet had to learn to live in a new place. At the end of his first school year, he is interviewed by a reporter for the school newspaper about his experiences in his first year in Chicago. Rajeet explains that some things about the two places are different and some things are the same. What does Rajeet find strange? What does Rajeet think about life in Chicago?

"Rajeet had no idea how different life would be."

FIRST READ

1　Lakeside Middle School welcomed a new student from Mumbai, India, this year. His name is Rajeet Basak. His first year in Chicago has been filled with **adjustments,** but Rajeet is happy. His experience has been **positive.**

2　In an **interview,** Rajeet explained how he learned about his family's move. "One day, I came home for dinner," Rajeet said. "During dinner, my father **announced** that we'd be moving to Chicago in a few weeks. I was in shock. I couldn't eat."

3　Rajeet had no idea how different life would be. In Chicago, at first he was lonely and sad about leaving his friends. But when October came, he could think of nothing but the cold. He knew neither how soon the real Chicago winter would begin nor how long it would last.

4　Rajeet said, "We knew it was colder here than in Mumbai, so my mom and I went shopping for a winter coat. It felt heavy and **bulky.** It was hard to move in. But I was glad to have it!"

5　One day Rajeet looked at the **thermometer.** He could not believe the reading was so low. And he could not believe that he saw snow falling. "I didn't know what was happening," Rajeet remembered. "I had read about snow. I'd never seen it. It was like soft white pillows, but I felt its cold bite when I touched it with bare hands. Now I always wear gloves lined with wool."

6　The weather was a shock to Rajeet, and the first weeks were lonely. However, Rajeet has new friends through his interest in sports. "Some sports are the same, but others are not. My friends and I still play soccer, however I call it 'football.' Here, there's another sport called 'football.' It is unlike anything I've ever seen!"

7 Rajeet added that school in Chicago was not hard to get used to. "In Mumbai, we had bigger classes. It's different here, but I've learned how things are done, and I like it. I've tried to be respectful to my teachers as we were in Mumbai and as my friends are here."

8 Rajeet also talked about food. "I like American food, but it's less spicy, and there's more meat. I like that some restaurants have a display of the food so you can see it before you order. However, my mother still makes the same things we ate in Mumbai. It's not hard to find Indian spices, and I love a dish of chicken curry. It tastes like my old life in Mumbai."

9 Rajeet has adapted to life in the U.S. and learns more every day. Next year he hopes to join the soccer team and hopes for a milder winter.

USING LANGUAGE CA-CCSS: ELD.PII.7.2.b.Ex

Create cohesion in each sentence by choosing the appropriate sequence word or phrase. Be sure your choice does not create an error or change the meaning of the sentence.

1. Rajeet moved from Mumbai, India, to Chicago, Illinois, and, _____, he was asked to give an interview to a newspaper about his experiences.

   ○ on the other hand
   ○ after a while
   ○ for example

2. There was a lot to get used to in the United States. _____, he could not believe how cold it was in Chicago during the winter.

   ○ For example
   ○ Finally
   ○ Next

3. It was difficult to wear a bulky winter coat. _____, Rajeet was grateful to have it.

   ○ Beforehand
   ○ For example
   ○ On the other hand

4. Rajeet still enjoyed sports as he did in India. _____, there were some differences between the sports that people played in both countries.

   ○ Finally
   ○ However
   ○ As a result

5. _____, Rajeet became comfortable with life in the United States and continues to learn more every day.

   ○ In the end
   ○ At first
   ○ Because

MEANINGFUL INTERACTIONS CA-CCSS: ELD.PII.7.1.Ex

Use the same chronological text structure as "A World Away" to discuss Rajeet's experiences in the United States. Then use the self-assessment rubric to evaluate your participation in the discussion.

- **First**, Rajeet and his family moved . . .

- **Soon after**, Rajeet discovered that the winters . . .

- As a result of touching snow, Rajeet **now** . . .

- **When** Rajeet learned about American sports, . . .

- **In addition**, he learned that American food . . .

- **At this time**, Rajeet feels . . .

 SELF-ASSESSMENT RUBRIC CA-CCSS: ELD.PII.7.1.Ex

	4 I did this well.	4 I did this pretty well.	2 I did this a little bit.	1 I did not do this.
I took an active part with others in doing the assigned task.				
I contributed effectively to the group's decisions.				
I understood the use of sequence words in the selection.				
I helped others understand the use of sequence words in the selection.				
I completed the sentences carefully and accurately to show the text sequence.				

Please note that excerpts and passages in the StudySync® library and this workbook are intended as touchstones to generate interest in an author's work. The excerpts and passages do not substitute for the reading of entire texts, and StudySync® strongly recommends that students seek out and purchase the whole literary or informational work in order to experience it as the author intended. Links to online resellers are available in our digital library. In addition, complete works may be ordered through an authorized reseller by filling out and returning to StudySync® the order form enclosed in this workbook.

Reading & Writing Companion 93

REREAD

Reread "A World Away." After you reread, complete the Using Language and Meaningful Interactions activities.

USING LANGUAGE   CA-CCSS: ELD.PII.7.4.Ex

Complete each sentence by choosing the noun that provides the correct information.

1. Rajeet experienced a cold _____ in Chicago.

   ○ winter
   ○ school

2. Rajeet thought his first winter _____ was just what he needed.

   ○ Rajeet
   ○ coat

3. After learning about American sports, Rajeet began to watch American football _____ on TV.

   ○ games
   ○ spices

4. Rajeet was used to Indian _____, but grew to enjoy American food, too.

   ○ food
   ○ lessons

5. Getting used to a new country is not easy, but _____ is learning new things every day.

   ○ Rajeet
   ○ people

MEANINGFUL INTERACTIONS CA-CCSS: ELD.PI.7.1.Ex, ELD.PI.7.6.a.Ex

The newspaper article "A World Away" describes Rajeet's experiences in the United States. Work with a partner or in a small group to discuss the ideas in the text. Then, use the self-assessment rubric to evaluate your participation in the discussion.

- In the article, Rajeet . . . life in Mumbai with life in Chicago.

- Chicago winters are . . . compared with . . .

- During Rajeet's first winter, he . . .

- Food in India and the United States is . . . because . . .

- Sports in India and in the United States are . . . For example, . . .

- Overall, Rajeet's comparisons lead to the conclusion that . . .

SELF-ASSESSMENT RUBRIC CA-CCSS: ELD.PI.7.1.Ex, ELD.PI.7.6.a.Ex

	4 I did this well.	3 I did this pretty well.	2 I did this a little bit.	1 I did not do this.
I explained my ideas clearly.				
I listened carefully to others' ideas.				
I spoke respectfully when disagreeing with others.				
I was courteous when sharing my ideas with others.				

REREAD

Reread "A World Away." After you reread, complete the Using Language and Meaningful Interactions activities.

⚙ USING LANGUAGE CA-CCSS: ELD.PII.7.4.Ex

Complete each sentence by choosing the noun phrase or noun clause that adds the correct details.

1. Rajeet experienced an _____ in Chicago.
   - ○ unbearably cold winter
   - ○ unbelievably mild winter

2. Rajeet thought his first _____ in the United States was just what he needed.
   - ○ lightweight but comfortable winter coat
   - ○ bulky but practical winter coat

3. After learning about American sports, Rajeet began to watch _____ on TV.
   - ○ American football games
   - ○ all kinds of sports

4. Rajeet was used to _____, but he grew to enjoy American food, too.
   - ○ the spicy food he ate in India
   - ○ the food he eats in the United States

5. Getting used to a new country is not easy, but Rajeet is learning _____ every day.
   - ○ amusing but useless new things
   - ○ life-changing and useful new things

👥 MEANINGFUL INTERACTIONS CA-CCSS: ELD.PI.7.3.Ex

The newspaper article "A World Away" describes Rajeet's new experiences being new in the United States. Express opinions about the text in a short discussion with classmates. Try to support your opinion and persuade others when you speak. Ask questions if something is unclear.

- I think Rajeet feels . . .

- The text supports this by . . .

- I agree with . . . , but . . .

- You may disagree that . . . , but . . .

- Wouldn't you agree that . . . ?

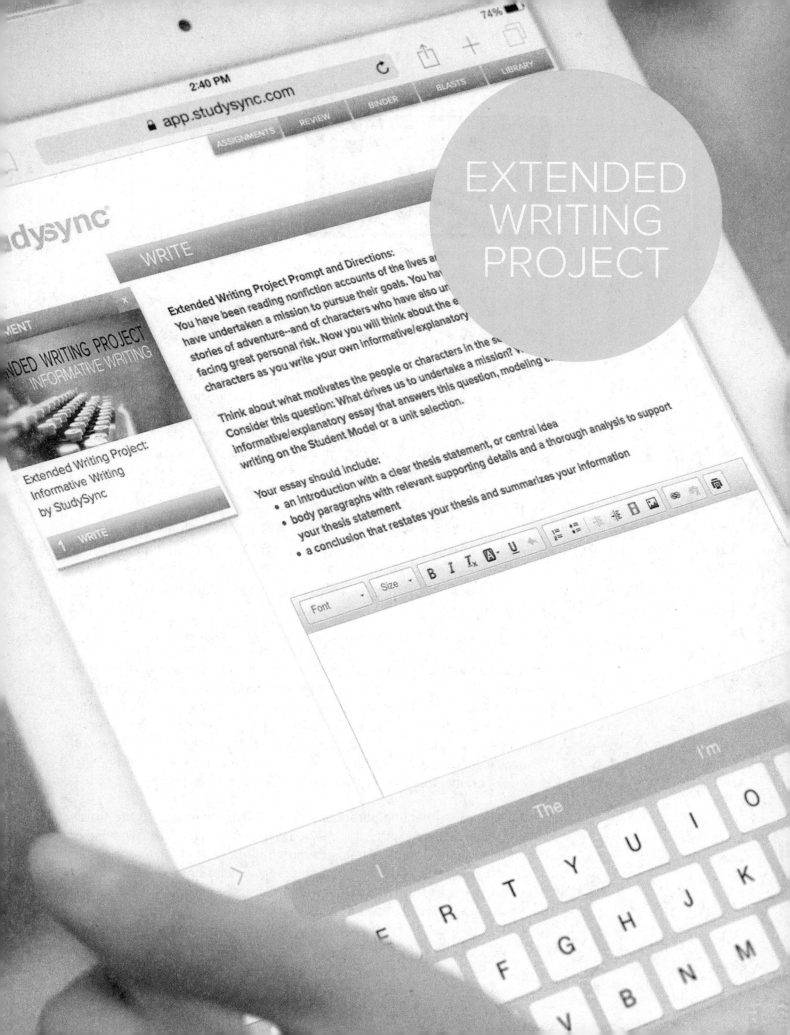

INFORMATIVE/ EXPLANATORY WRITING

WRITING PROMPT

You have been reading nonfiction accounts of the lives and experiences of real people who have undertaken a mission to pursue their goals. You have also been reading fictional stories of adventure—and of characters who have also undertaken missions, often while facing great personal risk. Now you will think about the experiences of these people and characters as you write your own informative/explanatory essay.

Your essay should include:

- an introduction with a clear thesis statement, or central idea
- body paragraphs with relevant supporting details and a thorough analysis to support your thesis statement
- a conclusion that restates your thesis and summarizes your information

An **informative/explanatory essay** examines a specific topic and conveys relevant information about it in a logical way. Informative/explanatory writing can explain, compare, define, describe, and inform about a topic. Some examples of informative writing include: printed and online newspaper, magazine, and encyclopedia articles; how-to manuals; full-length books on history, science, or any nonfiction topic; travel essays; pamphlets and public-service announcements; and professional Web pages and blogs.

Strong informative writing introduces a central (or main) idea in the thesis statement, and develops that central idea with supporting details. The use of transition words or phrases helps to direct the flow of ideas and to make connections between supporting details. The conclusion of an informative/ explanatory essay should come from the facts and information presented earlier in the essay. Because this type of essay is informative or explanatory, the writing should be unbiased. In other words, the writer does not state his or her own opinion but presents ideas that are based in fact. A good way the

Copyright © BookheadEd Learning, LLC

writer can do this is by establishing a formal style of writing. One reason the writer should include citations of sources is so that readers can double-check the ideas in the supporting details.

The features of informative/explanatory writing include:

- an introduction with a clear thesis statement
- a logical organizational structure in body paragraphs, indicated by transitions, formatting, and text features
- relevant supporting details
- precise language
- the citation of sources
- a concluding statement

As you continue with this extended writing project, you'll receive more instructions and practice to help you craft each of the elements of informative/explanatory writing in your own essay.

 STUDENT MODEL

Before you get started on your own informative/explanatory essay, begin by reading this essay that one student wrote in response to the writing prompt. As you read this Student Model, highlight and annotate the features of informative/explanatory writing that the student included in the essay.

Worth the Risk

It is impossible to know what drives people to take risks, but people do crazy, often dangerous, things when they undertake a mission. For example, Stanley Pearce walked thirty miles through the snow to stake a mining claim. Farah Ahmedi climbed a mountain on a prosthetic leg to reach freedom. Annie Johnson started a business from nothing but an idea so that she could support her children and not have others care for them. These real people had different reasons for doing what they did. Pearce wanted to strike it rich, while Ahmedi and Johnson were determined to survive desperate circumstances; however, all three shared an ability to endure hardship to accomplish their goals.

Stanley Pearce

Call of the Klondike by David Meissner and Kim Richardson is a true account of the Klondike Gold Rush. The text is based on primary sources, including the diary of Stanley Pearce, a gold miner. The authors describe the hardships that Pearce and other miners faced to pursue their dream of striking it rich. After sixty-eight miners arrived in Seattle, Washington, in 1897, weighed down with bags of precious gold dust, gold fever erupted. According to Meissner and Richardson, Pearce wrote that "every man who could raise the necessary funds for a year's grub stake was rushing...to start by the next boat for the promised land, where the dreams of all should be realized." Pearce's diaries reveal that the Klondike was not the "promised land" after all. The climate was harsh, and the gold was not plentiful. As a consequence, many miners became "engaged on schemes to fleece the unsuspecting" newcomers out of their money. Others were so desperate that they responded to rumors of gold by stampeding. Pearce describes one stampede that cost people their lives because they were not prepared for the frigid weather. Pearce's own fate is not clear, but he grew wiser from his experiences.

Farah Ahmedi

Unlike Stanley Pearce, who voluntarily went to the Klondike in search of fortune, Farah Ahmedi and her mother found themselves in a dire situation through no fault of their own. They were Afghans living in a war-torn city, and their only hope was to escape to Pakistan. By the time Ahmedi and her mother made it to the border, Pakistan had closed its gates to refugees. Ahmedi and her mother were now stranded in the desert. The situation was desperate. But Ahmedi was determined, so she learned the secret to getting across the border. It was to bribe the guards, but Ahmedi and her mother had no money. Fortunately, Ahmedi made friends with another family. The father, Ghulam Ali, had learned about a smuggler's pass over the mountains. He agreed to take Ahmedi and her mother through the pass, even though they were strangers. The path was dark and steep. According to Ahmedi, although she wore a prosthetic leg, she "hardly felt the exertion" because of her "desperation." It gave her "energy" and made her "forget the rigor of the climb." Ahmedi learned a different lesson from that of Stanley Pearce. She discovered that even during a crisis, there were kind people like Ghulam Ali. He not only helped save Ahmedi's life, but he also gave her hope in humanity.

Annie Johnson

Like Farah Ahmedi, Annie Johnson was a woman with a family and a fierce survival instinct. As a divorced African American woman with two children, Annie Johnson found herself in need of a job. As her granddaughter Maya Angelou explained in

Copyright © BookheadEd Learning, LLC

"New Directions," Johnson "decided to step off the road and cut me a new path." Instead of taking a job as a domestic or trying to get a job as a factory worker, Johnson devised an elaborate plan to cook meals for local mill and factory workers. Johnson's job was hard, and "business was slow," but she was determined to succeed in her mission. That meant "on balmy spring days, blistering summer noons, and cold, wet, and wintry middays," Johnson "never disappointed her customers." She planned her business carefully, and over time it grew into a successful store. Angelou credited her grandmother's drive and resolve for carrying her through hard times. She also suggested that Johnson's ability to handle only "unpalatable" choices with grace was the key to achieving her goals.

Pearce, Ahmedi, and Johnson all pursued their goals relentlessly and with good humor and grace, even when their situations became desperate. Pearce kept his common sense while others around him turned to schemes. Ahmedi managed to escape from a war-torn country. When she could not buy her way out of the situation, she found help from a compassionate man. Johnson became a successful businesswoman only after years of hard work. Each was driven to undertake a mission to become wealthy, to escape a war, to raise a family with dignity. Each had different levels of success, but all three learned from their experiences and passed the lessons along to those who came after them. We would all do well to learn from them.

THINK QUESTIONS

1. How does the writer compare and contrast the information about the motivations and goals of the three real people in the Student Model? Why does the writer use subheads to help organize the information? Cite specific evidence from the Student Model to support your answer.

2. How well does the writer use supporting details, such as facts, examples, anecdotes, and quotations, to develop the topic of taking risks to accomplish a goal? Cite specific details from the Student Model to support your response.

3. Write two or three sentences evaluating the writer's ending, or conclusion. Use specific evidence from the last paragraph of the Student Model.

4. Think about the writing prompt. Which selections or other resources would you use to write your own informative essay about two of the selections from the unit? Which two texts would you use? What topic would you want to explore and analyze? Create a list of the texts you might use for your prompt. Next, choose two texts on your list and cite one topic from each that interests you.

5. Based on the selections you have read, listened to, or researched, how would you answer the question, *What makes stories about why people undertake a mission so interesting to readers?* Which people and missions might you analyze in the informative essay you will be developing? Write a short paragraph that explains your answer.

PREWRITE

CA-CCSS: CA.W.7.5, CA.W.7.6, CA.SL.7.1b, CA.SL.7.1c, CA.SL.7.1d

WRITING PROMPT

You have been reading nonfiction accounts of the lives and experiences of real people who have undertaken a mission to pursue their goals. You have also been reading fictional stories of adventure—and of characters who have also undertaken missions, often while facing great personal risk. Now you will think about the experiences of these people and characters as you write your own informative/explanatory essay.

Your essay should include:

- an introduction with a clear thesis statement, or central idea
- body paragraphs with relevant supporting details and a thorough analysis to support your thesis statement
- a conclusion that restates your thesis and summarizes your information

You have been reading real and fictional stories about people and characters who have pursued their goals. In your extended writing project, you will explain how and why several of the people or characters from the unit texts drove themselves to undertake a mission. You will consider the steps they took to accomplish their mission to achieve their goals.

Because the topic of your informative/explanatory essay is about how and why people undertake a mission to pursue certain goals, you will want to consider the people and characters you have read about in the unit texts. Think about what their mission was and why they went after it. You might start by considering the experiences of Stanley Pearce, as described in *Call of the Klondike*. What was Pearce's goal? What drove him to pursue it? What steps did he take toward reaching his goal? How successful was Pearce? What, if anything, did he learn from undertaking his mission?

Make a list of the answers to these questions about Stanley Pearce and at least two other people or characters from other texts in the unit. As you write down your ideas, look for patterns that begin to emerge. Do the individuals' motivations or experiences have anything in common? Do you notice ideas or themes that are repeated? Looking for these patterns might help you form ideas to discuss in your own informative/explanatory essay. Use this model to help you get started with your own prewriting.

Text: *Call of the Klondike: A True Gold Rush Adventure,* by David Meissner and Kim Richardson

Person or Character: Stanley Pearce
Mission: To find gold and adventure in the Klondike
Motivation: To become rich
Steps Taken Toward Accomplishing Goal: Went to Klondike, staked a claim, endured hardship, lived through a "stampede"
Success at Accomplishing Goal: Not really; Pearce did not become wealthy because he did not find much gold.
What Person or Character Learned: Pearce became wise about how to survive in the frigid Klondike. He could have become a schemer or a thief, like many others, but he did not.

Please note that excerpts and passages in the StudySync® library and this workbook are intended as touchstones to generate interest in an author's work. The excerpts and passages do not substitute for the reading of entire texts, and StudySync® strongly recommends that students seek out and purchase the whole literary or informational work in order to experience it as the author intended. Links to online resellers are available in our digital library. In addition, complete works may be ordered through an authorized reseller by filling out and returning to StudySync® the order form enclosed in this workbook.

Reading & Writing
Companion
103

NOTES

SKILL:
THESIS
STATEMENT

DEFINE

The **thesis statement** (or thesis) is the most important sentence in an informative/explanatory essay because it tells what the writer is going to say about the essay's topic. The thesis statement expresses the writer's central or main idea about that topic—the position the writer will develop in the body of the essay. The thesis statement usually appears in the essay's introductory paragraph and is often the introduction's first or last sentence. In some essays, the writer hints at the thesis indirectly in the opening paragraph because he or she wants readers to determine the central idea on their own, after reading the text. By doing so, the author shows that he or she trusts the readers to infer the main point by comprehending the details. Whether the thesis is stated directly or indirectly, all the paragraphs in the essay should support the thesis statement (or central idea) with supporting details.

IDENTIFICATION AND APPLICATION

A thesis statement:

- makes a clear statement about the writer's central (or main) idea
- lets the reader know what to expect in the body of the essay
- responds fully and completely to an essay prompt
- is stated—or hinted at indirectly—in the introduction

MODEL

The following is the introduction paragraph from the Student Model, "Worth the Risk":

It is impossible to know what drives people to take risks, but people do crazy, often dangerous, things when they undertake a mission. For example,

Stanley Pearce walked thirty miles through the snow to stake a mining claim. Farah Ahmedi climbed a mountain on a prosthetic leg to reach freedom. Annie Johnson started a business from nothing but an idea so that she could support her children and not have others care for them. These real people had different reasons for doing what they did. **Pearce wanted to strike it rich, while Ahmedi and Johnson were determined to survive desperate circumstances; however, all three shared an ability to endure hardship to accomplish their goals.**

Notice the boldfaced thesis statement. This student's thesis statement responds to the prompt. It tells readers about the topic of the essay—what Pearce, Ahmedi, and Johnson wanted, or what their goals were. It also specifically states the writer's central (or main) idea about that topic. The writer asserts that Pearce, Ahmedi, and Johnson, "shared an ability to endure hardship to accomplish their goals."

PRACTICE

Write a thesis statement for your informative/explanatory essay that states your central idea in relation to the essay prompt. When you are finished, trade with a partner and offer each other constructive feedback. How clear is the writer's main point or idea? Is it obvious what this essay will focus on? Does it specifically address the writing prompt? Offer each other suggestions, and remember that your suggestions are most helpful when they are delivered with a positive attitude.

NOTES

Organize
ARGUMENTATIVE
WRITING

SKILL:
ORGANIZE
INFORMATIVE
WRITING

 ## DEFINE

The purpose of writing an informative/explanatory text is to inform readers. To do this effectively, writers need to organize and present their ideas, facts, details, and other information in a logical sequence that's easy to understand.

Experienced writers carefully choose an **organizational structure** that best suits their material. They often use an outline or another graphic organizer to determine which organizational (or text) structure will help them express their ideas effectively.

For example, scientific reports and studies often use a **cause-and-effect** text structure. This mirrors the information scientists need to relay—the experiment and the results of the experiment. Historians and writers of memoirs often use a **sequential** (or chronological) text structure, discussing events in the order in which they occurred. Other organizational structures include **problem and solution** and **compare and contrast.**

 ## IDENTIFICATION AND APPLICATION

- When selecting an organizational structure, writers must consider the purpose of their writing. They often ask themselves questions about the kind of information they are writing about. They might consider:
  › "What is the central idea I'd like to convey?"
  › "Would it make sense to relay events in the order they occurred?"
  › "Is there a specific problem discussed in the texts? What solutions seem likely answers to the problem?"
  › "Is there a natural cause and effect relationship in my information?"
  › "Can I compare and contrast different events or individuals' responses to events?"
  › "Am I teaching readers how to do something?"

NOTES

- Writers often use word choice to create connections and transitions between ideas and to suggest the organizational structure being used:
  › Sequential order: *first, next, then, finally, last, initially, ultimately*
  › Cause and effect: *because, accordingly, as a result, effect, so*
  › Compare and contrast: *like, unlike, also, both, similarly, although, while, but, however*

- Sometimes, within the overall structure, writers may find it necessary to organize individual paragraphs using other structures - a definition paragraph in a chronological structure, for instance. This should not affect the overall organization.

- Sometimes a writer may include special formatting elements in an informative/explanatory text if these are useful in clarifying organization. These elements may include headings, or phrases in bold that announce the start of a section of text. Headings are usually included only if called for in a prompt or when needed to guide a reader through a long or complex text.

 ## MODEL

The writer of the Student Model understood from her prewriting that she was mostly comparing and contrasting the life-changing experiences of three different people.

In this excerpt from the introduction in the Student Model, the writer makes the organizational structure clear by using cue (or signal) words:

> *Pearce wanted to strike it rich, **while** Ahmedi and Johnson were determined to survive desperate circumstances; however, all three shared an ability to endure hardship to accomplish their goals..*

The writer uses the words "while" and "however" to indicate contrasts. The first contrast, which uses the word "while," compares Pearce's mission with the missions of Ahmedi and Johnson. Then the writer uses "however" to indicate that even though all three individuals had a different mission, they shared something in common—an ability to endure hardship in trying to accomplish their goals.

The writer of the Student Model, "Worth the Risk," wanted to compare and contrast the missions and motivations of the three individuals. Therefore, the writer used a three-column chart to organize the ideas during the prewriting process. The writer color-coded the information to make clear which qualities or characteristics the individuals had in common. What was unique to each individual is unmarked.

STANLEY PEARCE	FARAH AHMEDI	ANNIE JOHNSON
wanted to find gold	was determined to survive	needed to support her family
was observant	had to support her family	started her own business
was able to fit in among the other miners	had to escape her homeland	had an ability to endure hardship
had an ability to endure hardship	was intelligent	was intelligent
learned from his experiences	was willing to ask for help	learned from her experiences
was intelligent	had an ability to endure hardship	made the best of a bad personal situation
discovered something unexpected about the way people act during tough times	learned from her experiences	choose her own way
	discovered something unexpected about the way people act during tough times	was an independent spirit
		was determined to survive

 PRACTICE

Use an *Organize Informative/Explanatory Writing* Three-Column Chart, such as the one you have just seen, to fill in the information you gathered in the Prewrite stage of writing your essay.

SKILL:
SUPPORTING
DETAILS

DEFINE

In informative/explanatory writing, writers develop their thesis statement with relevant information called **supporting details**. Relevant information can be any fact, definition, concrete detail, example, or quotation that is important to the reader's understanding of the topic and closely related to the thesis, or central idea. Supporting details can be found in a variety of places, but they must develop the thesis statement in order to be considered relevant and necessary:

- Facts important to understanding the topic
- Research related to the thesis statement
- Quotations from texts or from individuals such as experts or eyewitnesses
- Conclusions of scientific findings and studies
- Definitions from reference material

Writers can choose supporting details from many sources. Encyclopedias, research papers, newspaper articles, graphs, memoirs, biographies, criticism, documentaries, and online references can all provide relevant information for source material. Though information is plentiful and the source material varied, the writer must be careful to evaluate the quality of information to determine what information is most important and most closely related to the thesis statement. If the information doesn't support the topic, or if the information doesn't strengthen the writer's point, it is not relevant.

IDENTIFICATION AND APPLICATION

Step 1:

Review your thesis statement. To identify relevant supporting details, ask this question: What is my central or main idea about this topic? A writer might be making a statement about the value of team sports, for example:

Please note that excerpts and passages in the StudySync® library and this workbook are intended as touchstones to generate interest in an author's work. The excerpts and passages do not substitute for the reading of entire texts, and StudySync® strongly recommends that students seek out and purchase the whole literary or informational work in order to experience it as the author intended. Links to online resellers are available in our digital library. In addition, complete works may be ordered through an authorized reseller by filling out and returning to StudySync® the order form enclosed in this workbook.

Reading & Writing
Companion

109

Team sports help young players develop important skills they need in life.

Step 2:

Ask what a reader needs to know about the topic in order to understand the central idea. In order to understand a statement about how sports help players develop life skills, a reader must first know something about the specific sports and skills under discussion. He or she might write this sentence next:

Team sports, such as soccer and field hockey, provide opportunities for players to learn how to work together to meet a goal.

The writer then supplies the reason why:

Because in sports and in other areas of life, how you get to your goal is just as important as making the goal itself.

What could that possibly mean to a reader? The writer gives more information:

While reaching one's goals is highly valued in our society, we all need to remember that pursuing a goal requires hard work.

Step 3:

Look for facts, quotations, research, and the conclusions of others. They will strengthen the thesis statement. It is a building process. Build your information onto the information you gave in the sentence before. Identify supporting details. Carefully evaluate their relevance to your main idea. Ask yourself:

- Is this information necessary to the reader's understanding of the topic?
- Does this information help to prove my point?
- Does this information relate closely to my thesis statement?
- Is there stronger evidence that makes the same point?

 MODEL

The authors of *Call of the Klondike* had to determine which supporting details were most relevant to their topic—the harsh conditions experienced by miners during the Klondike Gold Rush. They included information from a reliable and valid source that would help readers understand what life was like for the miners.

NOTES

Staking a Claim

When prospectors found a promising spot, they staked a claim **by placing posts at each corner,** one **with their name and date** on it. The prospector then had **three days** to go to town and **file a legal claim.** Because the claims were usually measured by crude means, **disagreements over exact boundaries were common.**

The **first claim** in a new location was called the **"discovery claim."** **Subsequent claims** were **legally referred to by their relationship** to this claim, along with the name of the creek—**5 Above Eldorado, or 6 Below Bonanza,** for example.

—Museum at the Klondike Gold Rush National Historical Park, Seattle

Paragraph 1 briefly explains the process of staking a claim. The authors understand that many readers would not already know how gold miners secured their land. The supporting details (set in bold) identify the steps for the official process of recording a claim. The final sentence suggests that the process was not perfect. This detail directly supports the author's topic.

Paragraph 2 explains the difference between types of claims. It includes specific examples—"5 Above Eldorado or 6 Below Bonanza"—to illustrate the naming process. In case readers wonder where the information came from, the authors identify a reliable and valid source at the end of the paragraph—a museum in Seattle, Washington, devoted to the Klondike Gold Rush.

The details included in these two paragraphs are relevant to the topic and provide readers with evidence that shows that the process of claiming land, like life in the Klondike, was imperfect and could lead to confusion and conflict.

 PRACTICE

Using sources, write a few supporting details for your informative/explanatory essay that will help develop your thesis statement. List your details on a *Supporting Details* Relevancy Graphic Organizer to determine how strong your supporting details are. Then trade your details with a partner when you are finished. Offer feedback about the details. Engage in a peer review to determine which details are most relevant and strengthen your thesis statement.

PLAN

CA-CCSS: CA.W.7.2a, CA.W.7.2b, CA.W.7.5, CA.W.7.9a, CA.SL.7.1a, CA.SL.7.1c, CA.SL.7.2

WRITING PROMPT

You have been reading nonfiction accounts of the lives and experiences of real people who have undertaken a mission to pursue their goals. You have also been reading fictional stories of adventure—and of characters who have also undertaken missions, often while facing great personal risk. Now you will think about the experiences of these people and characters as you write your own informative/explanatory essay.

Your essay should include:

- an introduction with a clear thesis statement, or central idea
- body paragraphs with relevant supporting details and a thorough analysis to support your thesis statement
- a conclusion that restates your thesis and summarizes your information

Review the information you listed in your *Organize Informative/Explanatory Writing*

Three Column Chart listing three individuals and the details about their motivations and goals. Think about the best way to organize and present the details about the three individuals. This organized information and your thesis will help you to create a road map to use for writing your essay.

Consider the following questions as you develop the topics for your main paragraphs and their supporting details in the road map:

- What mission did each person or character undertake?
- What drove the individual to undertake the mission?
- How successful was the person or character in accomplishing the mission?

- Was the individual's goal a worthy or necessary one? Why or why not?
- What happened as a result of the process of pursuing the goal? Did each person or character change or learn anything important, even if he or she failed?
- What generalization can you make about undertaking a mission based on each individual's experience?

Use this model to get started with your road map:

Essay Road Map

Thesis statement: Pearce wanted to strike it rich, while Ahmedi and Johnson were determined to survive desperate circumstances; however, all three shared an ability to endure hardship to accomplish their goals.

Paragraph 1 Topic: Stanley Pearce

Supporting Detail #1: Like a lot of people, Pearce went to the Klondike to find gold and get rich quick, but soon figured out that the place was not "the promised land."

Supporting Detail #2: Pearce found the climate harsh and the people desperate, but instead of becoming like them, he observed the world around him and kept a diary.

Paragraph 2 Topic: Farah Ahmedi

Supporting Detail #1: Ahmedi needed to get herself and her mother out of their war-torn country, but they faced many obstacles, including a closed border and a lack of money.

Supporting Detail #2: Ahmedi made friends with another family, and together they found a way to escape; as a result, Ahmedi discovered that there were good people in the world.

Paragraph 3 Topic: Annie Johnson

Supporting Detail #1: Johnson had to take care of her family on her own, so she decided to take an unusual path—cooking meals for workers.

Supporting Detail #2: Despite many hardships, Johnson's drive and determination caused her to build a successful business that helped not only her children but also her grandchildren.

SKILL: INTRODUCTIONS

DEFINE

The **introduction** is the opening paragraph or section of a nonfiction text. In an informative/explanatory text, the introduction provides readers with important information by **introducing the topic** and **stating the thesis** that will be developed in the body of the text. A strong introduction also generates interest in the topic by engaging readers in an interesting or attentive way.

IDENTIFICATION AND APPLICATION

- In informative or explanatory writing, the introduction identifies the topic of the writing by explicitly stating what the text will be about. The writer may also use the introduction to provide some necessary background information about the topic to help the reader understand the information that is to come.

- In addition to the topic, the introduction includes the central, or main, idea that the writer will include in the text. This central (or main) idea is the **thesis statement.** A strong statement of the thesis serves as a guide for the remainder of the work. It lets the reader know what the focus of the essay is. The thesis statement should indicate the point the writer will make and the people or source materials he or she will discuss. Note, however, that a thesis is not always stated explicitly within the text. A writer might instead hint at the thesis through details and ideas in the introduction.

- It is customary to build interest in the topic by beginning the introduction with a **"hook,"** or a way to grab the reader's attention. This awakens the reader's natural curiosity and encourages him or her to read on. Hooks can ask open-ended questions, make connections to the reader or to life, or introduce a surprising fact.

MODEL

Take a look at the introduction of the text, *The Other Side of the Sky:*

> The gate to Pakistan was closed, and I could see that the Pakistani border guards were letting no one through. **People were pushing and shoving and jostling up against that gate, and the guards were driving them back. As we got closer, the crowd thickened, and I could hear the roar and clamor at the gate.** The Afghans were yelling something, and the Pakistanis were yelling back. My mother was clutching her side and gasping for breath, trying to keep up. **I felt desperate to get through, because the sun was setting, and if we got stuck here, what were we going to do?** Where would we stay? There was nothing here, no town, no hotel, no buildings, just the desert.

The writer begins with a **hook** in the form of some vivid details: People are pushing and shoving, and the crowd is roaring and clamoring at the gate. It is an effective hook because it makes readers wonder what is going on. They are likely to keep reading to find out what happens next.

The remainder of the paragraph from *The Other Side of the Sky* goes on to introduce the **topic:** the narrator's escape to Pakistan. The topic is suggested through the details of the narrator's thoughts as she stands at the gate to that country: "I felt desperate to get through, because the sun was setting, and if we got stuck here, what were we going to do?"

The **central idea,** however, is only hinted at in the introduction. The central idea of this passage focuses on the detail that the narrator is overcoming many challenges in order to escape from her war-torn homeland. However, there is no explicitly stated **thesis** here, because this is an excerpt from Farah Ahmedi's memoir, which is longer and more complex than an essay someone might write for school. The **thesis statement** for the entire book would be much longer than a sentence. The details in the introduction hint at the idea that the thesis might be about the courage and persistence it takes to survive a desperate situation.

 PRACTICE

Write an introduction for your informative essay that includes a hook, the topic, and the thesis statement. When you are finished, trade with a partner and offer each other feedback. How strong is the language of your partner's thesis statement? How clear is the topic? Were you hooked? Offer each other suggestions, and remember that suggestions are most helpful when they are constructive.

SKILL: BODY PARAGRAPHS AND TRANSITIONS

 DEFINE

Body paragraphs are the section of the essay between the introduction and the conclusion. This is where you support your thesis statement by developing your main points with evidence from the text and analysis. Typically, each body paragraph will focus on one main point or idea to avoid confusing the reader. The main point of each body paragraph must support the thesis statement.

It's important to structure your body paragraph clearly. One strategy for structuring the body paragraph for an informational essay is the following:

Topic sentence: The topic sentence is the first sentence of your body paragraph and clearly states the main point of the paragraph. It's important that your topic sentence develop the main assertion or statement you made in your thesis statement.

Evidence #1: It's important to support your topic sentence with evidence. Evidence can be relevant facts, definitions, concrete details, quotations, or other information and examples.

Analysis/Explanation #1: After presenting evidence to support your topic sentence, you will need to analyze that evidence and explain how it supports your topic sentence and, in effect, your thesis statement.

Evidence #2: Continue to develop your topic sentence with a second piece of evidence.

Analysis/Explanation #2: Analyze this second piece of evidence and explain how it supports your topic sentence and, in effect, your thesis.

Concluding sentence: After presenting your evidence you need to wrap up your main idea and transition to the next paragraph in your conclusion sentence.

Transitions are connecting words and phrases that clarify the relationships between (or among) ideas in a text. Transitions work at three different levels: within a sentence, between paragraphs, and to indicate organizational structure.

Authors of informative/explanatory texts use transitions to help readers recognize the overall organizational structure. Transitions also help readers make connections between (or among) ideas within and across sentences and paragraphs. Also, by adding transition words or phrases to the beginning or end of a paragraph, authors guide readers smoothly through the text.

In addition, transition words and phrases help authors make connections between (or among) words within a sentence. Conjunctions such as *and, or,* and *but* and prepositions such as *with, beyond, inside,* show the relationships between (or among) words. Transitions help readers understand how words fit together to make meaning.

 IDENTIFICATION AND APPLICATION

- Body paragraphs are the section of the essay between the introduction and conclusion. Body paragraphs provide the evidence and analysis/explanation needed to support the thesis statement. Typically, writers develop one central idea per body paragraph.
  › Topic sentences clearly state the central (or main) idea of the paragraph.
  › Evidence consists of relevant facts, definitions, concrete details, quotations, or other information and examples.
  › Analysis and explanation are needed to explain how the evidence supports the topic sentence.
  › The concluding sentence wraps up the main point and transitions to the next body paragraph.

- Transition words or phrases are a necessary element of a successful piece of informative writing.
  › Transition words help readers understand the organizational structure of an informative text. Here are some transition words or phrases that are frequently used in three different organizational (or text) structures:
    › Cause-effect: *because, since, as a result, effect, so, for, since, if . . . then*
    › Compare-contrast: *like, also, both, similarly, in the same way* to compare; *although, while, but, yet, however, whereas, on the contrary, on the other hand* to contrast
    › Chronological (sequential, or time) order: *first, next, then, finally, last, soon, later, meanwhile, in the meantime*

 NOTES

> Transition words help readers understand the flow of ideas and concepts in a text. Some of the most useful transitions are words that indicate that the ideas in one paragraph are building on (or adding to) those in another. Examples include: *furthermore, therefore, in addition, moreover.*

MODEL

The Student Model uses a body paragraph structure to develop the central ideas presented in the thesis statement. It also uses transitions to help the reader understand the relationship between (or among) ideas in the text.

Read the body paragraphs from the Student Model, "Worth the Risk." Look closely at the structure and note the transition words in bold. Think about the purpose of the information presented. Does it effectively develop the main points made in each topic sentence? How do the transition words help you understand the similarities and differences among these three individuals and their experiences?

Stanley Pearce

Call of the Klondike by David Meissner and Kim Richardson is a true account of the Klondike Gold Rush. The text is based on primary sources, including the diary of Stanley Pearce, a gold miner. The authors describe the hardships that Pearce and other miners faced to pursue their dream of striking it rich. After sixty-eight miners arrived in Seattle, Washington, in 1897, weighed down with bags of precious gold dust, gold fever erupted. According to Meissner and Richardson, Pearce wrote that "every man who could raise the necessary funds for a year's grub stake was rushing...to start by the next boat for the promised land, where the dreams of all should be realized." Pearce's diaries reveal that the Klondike was not the "promised land" after all. The climate was harsh, and the gold was not plentiful. As a consequence, many miners became "engaged on schemes to fleece the unsuspecting" newcomers out of their money. Others were so desperate that they responded to rumors of gold by stampeding. Pearce describes one stampede that cost people their lives because they were not prepared for the frigid weather. Pearce's own fate is not clear, but he grew wiser from his experiences.

Farah Ahmedi

Unlike Stanley Pearce, who voluntarily went to the Klondike in search of fortune, Farah Ahmedi and her mother found themselves in a dire situation through no fault of their own. They were Afghans living in a war-torn city, and their only hope was to escape to Pakistan. By the time Ahmedi and her mother made it to the border, Pakistan had closed its gates to refugees. Ahmedi and her mother were now stranded in the desert. The situation was desperate. But Ahmedi was determined, so she learned the secret to getting across the border. People were bribing the guards to let them into Pakistan, but she and her mother had no money. Then Ahmedi made friends with another family. The father, Ghulam Ali, learned about a smuggler's pass over the mountains. He agreed to bring Ahmedi and her mother along, even though they were strangers. The path was dark and steep. According to Ahmedi, although she wore a prosthetic leg, she "hardly felt the exertion" because of her "desperation." It gave her "energy" and made her "forget the rigor of the climb." Ahmedi learned a different lesson from that of Stanley Pearce. She discovered that even during a crisis, there were kind people like Ghulam Ali. He not only helped save Ahmedi's life but also gave her hope in humanity.

Annie Johnson

Like Farah Ahmedi, Annie Johnson was a woman with a family and a fierce survival instinct. As a divorced African American woman with two children, Annie Johnson found herself in need of a job. As her granddaughter Maya Angelou explained in "New Directions," Johnson "decided to step off the road and cut me a new path." Instead of taking a job as a domestic or trying to get a job as a factory worker, Johnson devised an elaborate plan to cook meals for local mill and factory workers. Johnson's job was hard, and "business was slow," but she was determined to succeed in her mission. That meant "on balmy spring days, blistering summer noons, and cold, wet, and wintry middays," Johnson "never disappointed her customers." She planned her business carefully, and over time it grew into a successful store. Angelou credited her grandmother's drive and resolve for carrying her through hard times. She also suggested that Johnson's ability to handle only "unpalatable" choices with grace was the key to the success of her mission.

Please note that excerpts and passages in the StudySync® library and this workbook are intended as touchstones to generate interest in an author's work. The excerpts and passages do not substitute for the reading of entire texts, and StudySync® strongly recommends that students seek out and purchase the whole literary or informational work in order to experience it as the author intended. Links to online resellers are available in our digital library. In addition, complete works may be ordered through an authorized reseller by filling out and returning to StudySync® the order form enclosed in this workbook.

Reading & Writing Companion   119

Pearce, Ahmedi, and Johnson all pursued their goals relentlessly and with good humor and grace, even when their situations became desperate. Pearce kept his common sense while others around him turned to schemes. Ahmedi managed to escape from a war-torn country. When she could not buy her way out of the situation, she found help from a compassionate man. Johnson became a successful businesswoman only after years of hard work. Each was driven to undertake a mission to become wealthy, to escape a war, to raise a family with dignity. Each had different levels of success, but all three learned from their experiences and passed the lessons along to those who came after them. We would all do well to learn from them.

In previous lessons, you have learned about the thesis of the Student Model essay, which was stated clearly in the introduction: While Pearce, Ahmedi, and Johnson had different motivations, "all three shared an ability to endure hardship to accomplish their goals." Keep that thesis in mind as you consider the body paragraphs.

The first two sentences of body paragraph 1 of the Student Model provide background information about the source text *Call of the Klondike*. The third sentence states that "The authors describe the hardships that Pearce and other miners faced to pursue their dream of striking it rich." This **topic sentence** clearly establishes the central (or main) idea this body paragraph will develop. The writer will attempt to show how hard life was for miners in the Klondike despite—or because of—their efforts to become rich quickly.

This topic sentence is immediately followed by **evidence.** The writer uses details and quotations from the source text to explain how many people had high hopes of striking it rich in the Klondike, but their dreams quickly soured because the Klondike was not the "promised land." The writer explains that instead of finding riches, many miners turned to scheming or desperate stampeding. The paragraph **concludes** with an **analysis** of Pearce's character: "he not only grew wiser from his experiences, he also became a keen observer of human nature."

All three body paragraphs use **transitional words** strategically to show relationships between the main points in each body paragraph. The first sentence of the second body paragraph states "**Unlike** Stanley Pearce …. Farah Ahmedi and her mother found themselves in a dire situation through no fault of their own." The transitional word "unlike" makes it clear that the writer is highlighting an important contrast or point of difference between Pearce and Ahmedi.

The writer also uses transition words such as "but," "because," and "although" within the body paragraphs themselves to help guide readers as they transition from one sentence to the next.

 PRACTICE

Write one body paragraph for your informative essay that follows the suggested format. When you are finished, trade with a partner and offer each other feedback. How effective is the topic sentence at stating the main point of the paragraph? How strong is the evidence used to support the topic sentence? Are all quotes and paraphrased evidence cited properly? Did the analysis thoroughly support the topic sentence? Offer each other suggestions, and remember that suggestions are most helpful when they are constructive.

CONCLUSIONS

sync•skills

SKILL:
CONCLUSIONS

 DEFINE

The **conclusion** is the final paragraph or section of a nonfiction text. In an informative/explanatory text, the conclusion brings the discussion to a close. It follows directly from the introduction and body of the text by referring back to the main ideas presented there. A conclusion should reiterate the thesis statement and summarize the main ideas covered in the body of the text. Depending on the type of text, a conclusion might also include a recommendation or solution, a call to action, or an insightful statement. Many conclusions try to connect with readers by encouraging them to apply what they have learned from the text to their own lives.

 IDENTIFICATION AND APPLICATION

- An effective informative conclusion reinforces the thesis statement.

- An effective informative conclusion briefly mentions or reviews the strongest supporting facts or details. This reminds readers of the most relevant information and evidence in the work.

- The conclusion leaves the reader with a final thought. In informative writing, this final thought may:
  › answer a question posed by the introduction
  › ask a question on which the reader can reflect
  › ask the reader to take action on an issue
  › present a last, compelling example
  › convey a memorable or inspiring message
  › spark curiosity and encourage readers to learn more about the topic

MODEL

In the concluding paragraph of the student model, "Worth the Risk," the writer reinforces the thesis statement, reminds the reader of relevant details, and ends with a final thought.

> *Pearce, Ahmedi, and Johnson all pursued their goals relentlessly and with good humor and grace, even when their situations became desperate. Pearce kept his common sense while others around him turned to schemes. Ahmedi managed to escape from a war-torn country.* When she could not buy her way out of the situation, she found help from a compassionate man. *Johnson became a successful businesswoman only after years of hard work. Each was driven to undertake a mission to become wealthy, to escape a war, to raise a family. Each had different levels of success, but all three learned from their experiences and passed the lessons along to those who came after them. We would all do well to learn from them.*

According to the thesis statement, even though Pearce, Ahmedi, and Johnson had different motivations for pursuing their mission, they shared the ability to endure hardship. The first line of the conclusion links back to that idea by reminding readers of the challenges that the three individuals faced as they pursued their mission. Relevant facts in the next few sentences highlight each individual's goal. Then the writer states that all three individuals "were driven to undertake a mission—to become wealthy, to escape a war, to raise a family. "Each had different levels of success, but all three learned from their experiences and passed the lessons along to those who came after them." These two sentences emphasize how the individuals were both different yet similar. They explicitly support the thesis of the essay. Finally, the writer concludes with a recommendation. The writer states, "We would all do well to learn from them." The writer is encouraging readers to learn from the experiences of others.

 PRACTICE

Write a conclusion for your informative essay. When you are finished, trade with a partner and offer each other feedback. How effectively did the writer restate the main points of the essay in the conclusion? What final thought did the writer leave you with? Offer each other suggestions, and remember that they are most helpful when they are constructive.

DRAFT

CA-CCSS: CA.RI.7.1, CA.W.7.2a, CA.W.7.2b, CA.W.7.2d, CA.W.7.2e, CA.W.7.4, CA.W.7.5, CA.W.7.6, CA.SL.7.1a, CA.SL.7.1.b, CA.SL.7.1c, CA.SL.7.1d, CA.SL.7.2, CA.SL.7.6, CA.L.7.3

WRITING PROMPT

You have been reading nonfiction accounts of the lives and experiences of real people who have undertaken a mission to pursue their goals. You have also been reading fictional stories of adventure—and of characters who have also undertaken missions, often while facing great personal risk. Now you will think about the experiences of these people and characters as you write your own informative/explanatory essay.

Your essay should include:

- an introduction with a clear thesis statement, or central idea
- body paragraphs with relevant supporting details and a thorough analysis to support your thesis statement
- a conclusion that restates your thesis and summarizes your information

You have already made progress toward writing your own informative/ explanatory text. You have thought about your purpose, audience, and topic. You've carefully examined the unit's texts and selected the people or characters about whom you want to write. Based on your analysis of textual evidence, you've identified what you want to say about their motivations for undertaking a mission. You've decided how to organize information and gathered supporting details. Now it's time to write a draft of your essay.

Use your outline and your other prewriting materials to help you as you write. Remember that informative writing begins with an introduction and presents a thesis statement. Body paragraphs develop the thesis statement with supporting ideas, details, examples, quotations, and other relevant information and explanations drawn from the texts. Transition words and phrases help the reader follow the flow of information and understand the relationship between (or among) ideas. A concluding paragraph restates or reinforces

Copyright © BookheadEd Learning, LLC

your thesis statement. An effective conclusion can also do more—it can leave a lasting impression on your readers.

When drafting, ask yourself these questions:

- How can I improve my hook to make it more appealing?
- What can I do to clarify my thesis statement?
- What textual evidence—including relevant facts, strong details, and interesting quotations in each body paragraph—supports my thesis statement?
- Would more precise language or different details about these extraordinary individuals make the text more exciting and vivid?
- How well have I communicated what these individuals experienced and achieved?
- What final thought do I want to leave with my readers?

Before you submit your draft, read it over carefully. You want to be sure that you've responded to all aspects of the prompt.

REVISE

CA-CCSS: CA.RI.7.1, CA.W.7.2a, CA.W.7.2b, CA.W.7.2c, CA.W.7.2d. CA.W.7.2e, CA.W.7.2f, CA.W.7.4. CA.W.7.5. CA.W.7.6, CA.W.7.9a, CA.SL.7.1a. CA.SL.7.1c. CA.L.7.3a

WRITING PROMPT

You have been reading nonfiction accounts of the lives and experiences of real people who have undertaken a mission to pursue their goals. You have also been reading fictional stories of adventure—and of characters who have also undertaken missions, often while facing great personal risk. Now you will think about the experiences of these people and characters as you write your own informative/explanatory essay.

Your essay should include:

- an introduction with a clear thesis statement, or central idea
- body paragraphs with relevant supporting details and a thorough analysis to support your thesis statement
- a conclusion that restates your thesis and summarizes your information

You have written a draft of your informative/explanatory essay. You have also received input from your peers about how to improve it. Now you are going to revise your draft.

Here are some recommendations to help you revise.

- Review the suggestions made by your peers.
- Focus on maintaining a formal style. A formal style suits your purpose—giving information about a serious topic. It also fits your audience—students, teachers, and other readers interested in learning more about your topic.
  › As you revise, eliminate any slang.

NOTES

> Remove any first-person pronouns such as "I," "me," or "mine" or instances of addressing readers as "you." These are more suitable to a writing style that is informal, personal, and conversational. Check that you have used all pronouns correctly.
> If you include your personal opinions, remove them. Your essay should be clear, direct, and unbiased.

- After you have revised elements of style, think about whether there is anything else you can do to improve your essay's information or organization.

  > Have you clearly stated your thesis statement in your introduction? Does it make your audience and purpose clear? Does it let readers know your central idea about the topic?
  > Do you need to add any new textual evidence to support your thesis statement or engage your readers' interest? For example, is there a detail about one individual's experiences that readers will find fascinating or with which they can identify?
  > Did one of your subjects say anything interesting that you forgot to quote? Quotations can add life to your essay. Be sure to cite your sources.
  > Can you substitute a more precise word for a word that is general or overused? Precise language will make your writing more interesting to read.
  > Consider your organization. Would your essay flow better if you used specific transitions to indicate the connections between (or among) ideas in your paragraphs?

Please note that excerpts and passages in the StudySync® library and this workbook are intended as touchstones to generate interest in an author's work. The excerpts and passages do not substitute for the reading of entire texts, and StudySync® strongly recommends that students seek out and purchase the whole literary or informational work in order to experience it as the author intended. Links to online resellers are available in our digital library. In addition, complete works may be ordered through an authorized reseller by filling out and returning to StudySync® the order form enclosed in this workbook.

SKILL: SOURCES
AND CITATIONS

 DEFINE

Sources are the documents and information that an author uses to research his or her writing. Some sources are **primary sources.** A primary source is a firsthand account of thoughts or events by the individual who experienced or witnessed them. Other sources are **secondary sources.** A secondary source analyzes and interprets primary sources. **Citations** are notes that give information about the sources an author used in his or her writing. Citations are required whenever authors quote the words of other people or refer to their ideas in writing. Citations let readers know who originally came up with those words and ideas.

 IDENTIFICATION AND APPLICATION

- Sources can be primary or secondary in nature. Primary sources are firsthand accounts, artifacts, or other original materials. Examples of primary sources include:
  - › Letters or other correspondence
  - › Photographs
  - › Official documents
  - › Diaries or journals
  - › Autobiographies or memoirs
  - › Eyewitness accounts or interviews
  - › Audio recordings and radio broadcasts
  - › Works of art
  - › Artifacts

- Secondary sources are usually text. Secondary sources are the written interpretation and analysis of primary source materials. Some examples of secondary sources include:
  - › Encyclopedia articles
  - › Textbooks

- › Commentary or criticism
- › Histories
- › Documentary films
- › News analyses

- Whether sources are primary or secondary, they must be **credible** and **accurate.** Writers of informative/explanatory texts look for sources from experts in the topic about which they are writing.

  - › When researching online, writers should look for URLs that contain ".gov" (government agencies), ".edu" (colleges and universities), and ".org" (museums and other nonprofit organizations).
  - › Writers also use respected print and online news and information sources.

- Anytime a writer uses words from another source exactly as they are written, the words must appear in quotation marks. Quotation marks show that the words are not the writer's own words but are borrowed from another source. In the Student Model, the writer used quotation marks around words taken directly from the source, *Call of the Klondike:*

  > *According to Meissner and Richardson, Pearce wrote that* **"every man who could raise the necessary funds for a year's grub stake was rushing…to start by the next boat for the promised land, where the dreams of all should be realized."**

- A writer includes a citation to give credit to any source, whether primary or secondary, that is quoted exactly. There are several different ways to cite a source.

  - › One way to give credit is to cite the source of the quotation in the context of the sentence. This is what the writer of the Student Model does in the example above. The writer identifies the authors of the secondary source, who in turn quoted from Stanley Pearce's diary, a primary source.
  - › Another way is to put the author's last name and the page number in parenthesis at the end of the sentence in which the quote appears.
  - › Be sure to ask your teacher which citation style he or she prefers.

- Citations are also necessary when a writer borrows ideas from another source, even if the writer paraphrases, or puts those ideas in his or her own words. Citations credit the source, but they also help readers discover where they can learn more.

Please note that excerpts and passages in the StudySync® library and this workbook are intended as touchstones to generate interest in an author's work. The excerpts and passages do not substitute for the reading of entire texts, and StudySync® strongly recommends that students seek out and purchase the whole literary or informational work in order to experience it as the author intended. Links to online resellers are available in our digital library. In addition, complete works may be ordered through an authorized reseller by filling out and returning to StudySync® the order form enclosed in this workbook.

Reading & Writing Companion   129

NOTES

MODEL

In this excerpt from the Student Model essay, the writer uses quotations from secondary source material. The writer identifies the source by name at the beginning of the paragraph.

> Like Farah Ahmedi, Annie Johnson was a woman with a family and a fierce survival instinct. As a divorced African American woman with two children, Annie Johnson found herself in need of a job. As her granddaughter Maya Angelou explained in "New Directions," Johnson **"decided to step off the road and cut me a new path."** Instead of taking a job as a domestic or trying to get a job as a factory worker, Johnson devised an elaborate plan to cook meals for local mill and factory workers. Johnson's job was hard, and **"business was slow,"** but she was determined to succeed in her mission. That meant **"on balmy spring days, blistering summer noons, and cold, wet, and wintry middays,"** Johnson **"never disappointed her customers."** She planned her business carefully, and over time it grew into a successful store. Angelou credited her grandmother's drive and resolve for carrying her through hard times. She also suggested that Johnson's ability to handle only "unpalatable" choices with grace was the key to the success of her mission.

Notice that each sentence begins with the writer's own words. When the writer uses portions of text from the source material, that text appears in quotation marks. The student has cited the author Maya Angelou at the beginning of the paragraph. The writer assumes that readers will understand that all the quotations in the paragraph are from Angelou.

Because the cited text is written by Angelou about her grandmother Annie Johnson, and not by Johnson herself, it is a secondary source. All references to the secondary source should be cited, to give credit to the author.

PRACTICE

Include citations for all quoted information in your informative/explanatory essay. When you are finished, trade with a partner and offer each other feedback. How thorough was the writer in citing sources for the essay? Offer each other suggestions, and remember that they are most helpful when they are constructive. You may need to search online for each text you cite to gather its complete bibliographic information (author, date of publication, publisher, city). Jot down this information on notecards for easy reference.

NOTES

EDIT, PROOFREAD, AND PUBLISH

CA-CCSS: CA.W.7.2a, CA.W.7.2b, CA.W.7.2c, CA.W.7.2d, CA.W.7.2e, CA.W.7.2f, CA.W.7.4, CA.W.7.5, CA.W.7.6, CA.W.7.9a, CA.SL.7.1c, CA.SL.7.4, CA.SL.7.5, CA.SL.7.6, CA.L.7.1a, CA.L.7.1b, CA.L.7.1c, CA.L.7.2a, CA.L.7.2b, CA.L.7.3a, CA.L.7.4b, CA.L.7.4c, CA.L.7.4d, CA.L.7.6

WRITING PROMPT

You have been reading nonfiction accounts of the lives and experiences of real people who have undertaken a mission to pursue their goals. You have also been reading fictional stories of adventure—and of characters who have also undertaken missions, often while facing great personal risk. Now you will think about the experiences of these people and characters as you write your own informative/explanatory essay.

Your essay should include:

- an introduction with a clear thesis statement, or central idea
- body paragraphs with relevant supporting details and a thorough analysis to support your thesis statement
- a conclusion that restates your thesis and summarizes your information

You have revised your informative/explanatory essay and received input from your peers on that revision. Now it's time to edit and proofread your essay to produce a final version. Have you included all the valuable suggestions from your peers? Ask yourself: Have I fully developed my thesis statement with strong textual evidence? Do my transitions lead to a natural flow of ideas? Do my word choices and writing style reflect the needs of my audience and purpose? Does my conclusion fully summarize the main ideas in my essay? Have I accurately cited my sources? What more can I do to improve my essay's information and organization?

When you are satisfied with your work, move on to proofread it for errors. For example, have you used correct punctuation for quotations and citations? Have you made sure you used commas correctly to separate coordinate adjectives and to set off phrases and clauses in your compound, complex, and compound-complex sentences? Have you used specialized vocabulary and technical terms correctly? Be sure to correct any misspelled words.

Once you have made all your corrections, you are ready to submit and publish your work. You can distribute your writing to family and friends, place it on a bulletin board, or post it on your blog. If you publish online, create links to your sources and citations. That way, readers can follow up on what they have learned from your essay and read more about your topic.

Text Fulfillment
Through StudySync

If you are interested in specific titles, please fill out the form below and we will check availability through our partners.

ORDER DETAILS

Date:

TITLE	AUTHOR	Paperback/ Hardcover	Specific Edition *If Applicable*	Quantity

SHIPPING INFORMATION

Contact:

Title:

School/District:

Address Line 1:

Address Line 2:

Zip or Postal Code:

Phone:

Mobile:

Email:

BILLING INFORMATION   ☐ *SAME AS SHIPPING*

Contact:

Title:

School/District:

Address Line 1:

Address Line 2:

Zip or Postal Code:

Phone:

Mobile:

Email:

PAYMENT INFORMATION

☐ CREDIT CARD

Name on Card:

Card Number: Expiration Date: Security Code:

☐ PO

Purchase Order Number:

StudySync Text Fulfillment, BookheadEd Learning, LLC
610 Daniel Young Drive | Sonoma, CA 95476